Knowledge and Truth

*Reflections on the Problems of Human
Knowledge and Contemporary Alternatives
to Traditional Epistemology*

Humphrey Uchenna Ani, PhD

Foreword by Prof Amechi Udefi

Knowledge and Truth

Knowledge and Truth: Reflections on the Problems of Human Knowledge and Contemporary Alternatives to Traditional Epistemology.

Copyright © 2025 by Humphrey Uchenna Ani, PhD.

All rights reserved.

No part of this book may be reproduced or used in any manner whatsoever without the express written permission of the publisher except for the use of brief quotations in a book review.

Published in the United States of America by:

www.btbpublishing.com

Available wherever books are sold or at: www.blackbooksplus.com

ISBN: 978-1-63652-396-5 (Paperback)

Library of Congress Control Number in-pub-data

Dedication

Bigard Memorial Seminary, Enugu, Nigeria

Lonergan Institute, Boston College, Massachusetts, USA

Saint John Vianney College Seminary, Miami, Florida, USA

Acknowledgments

I am grateful to God for the inspiration and good health during the research and writing of this work on *Knowledge and Truth*. My academic communities in Bigard Memorial Seminary, Enugu, and the Flanagan House of the Lonergan Institute, Boston College, Massachusetts, gave me the scholarly and conducive disposition to complete this work. I owe them immense gratitude. This work started in Bigard, Enugu, and was completed at Boston College, thanks to the post-doctoral fellowship the Lonergan Institute of Boston College offered me. This fellowship program was a transformative experience, introducing me to friends and scholars like Jeremy Wilkins, Pat Byrne, Mary Elliot, Kerry Cronin, Ann McInerney, Joseph Mwongi, Don Giadio de Biasio, Christian Krokus, Joan, and Strad Engler, who helped to shape my ideas on the topics discussed. Thank you all for making my Boston experience genuinely enriching.

Furthermore, I owe much gratitude to my Boston "brothers": Modestus Onwumelu, Edmund Ugwoegbu, Anthony Mecha, Joseph Akilo, Chrysantus Ugorji, and Toni Nweke. They helped me in the final days of this work. I would like to express my profound gratitude to Prof. Amechi Udefi of the University of Ibadan, Nigeria, whose guidance and insightful feedback significantly shaped the ideas and formation of thoughts in this work. As a seasoned professor of philosophy, he played a crucial role in restructuring the initial order of the work and creatively critiquing some of my ideas, which led to several cancellations and corrections before this work crystallized into its current form. I learned a great deal from his mastery amendments. His ideas on African epistemology provided the initial block of thoughts that led me to discuss the alternatives to traditional epistemology. I am also thankful to him for agreeing to write the foreword for this work during his research leave in Ghana.

I am truly fortunate to have brilliant scholars like Joseph Ogbonnaya, Stan Chu Ilo, and Joseph Ezechi as friends. Their intelligent criticisms and corrections have been instrumental in sustaining my academic activities, and for this, I am deeply grateful. The members of staff of the philosophy department of Bigard and some of my students like Isaiah Jideoffor Abba, Stanley Eme, Stephen Orike, Uche Anioke, and Amaka Ngwu, who helped to format and organize the work, are also deserving of my heartfelt thanks for their roles in this academic project.

I am particularly grateful to Martha Ugwu, who dedicated her time to work on the grammatical part of the work. To my family and friends: Max Laru Ngene, Anthony Ude, Paschal Ekediegwu and Stan C. Zeowa, and many others, whom I cannot mention here for want of space, I owe you all tremendous gratitude.

Finally, I thank the staff and students of Saint John Vianney College Seminary, Miami, Florida, especially our President and Rector, Msgr, Pablo Navarro and Prof. O.D Alexander, whose assistance and intelligent mentorship shaped the final form of this work. Your unwavering support and encouragement have provided me with an excellent inspiration and disposition to write this book: *Knowledge and Truth*. God bless you all.

TABLE OF CONTENTS

Dedication

Acknowledgments

FOREWORD

INTRODUCTION

Part One: Human Knowledge

Chapter One: **The Meaning of Human Knowledge**

1.1 Etymology of Human Knowledge

1.2 Knowledge as Consciousness

1.3 Theoretical Explanation of Knowledge

Chapter Two: **The Problems of Human Knowledge**

2.1 What Constitutes the Problems of Human Knowledge?

2.2 Perspectives on the Problems of Human Knowledge

2.3 Implications of Problems of Human Knowledge

Part Two: Core Elements of Human Knowledge

Chapter Three: **Belief, Justification and Truth**

3.1 Relationship of Knowledge to Belief, Justification and Truth

3.2 Knowledge and Belief

3.3 Types of Belief

3.4 Schools of Thought on Belief

3.4.1 Representationalism

3.4.2 Functionalism

3.4.3 Dispositionalism

3.4.4 Interpretationism

Chapter Four: **Knowledge and Justification**

4.1 The Idea of Justification

4.2 Is Knowledge Justified True Belief?

4.3 Justified True Belief (JTB)

4.4 The Gettier Problem

4.5 The First Gettier Case and Gettier-Type Examples

4.6 Explanations of Gettier's Case and Gettier-Type Examples

4.7 Attempted Solutions to the Gettier Problem

Chapter Five: **Knowledge and Truth**

5.1 What is Truth?

5.2 Truth in Epistemology

5.3 Practical Values of Truth

5.4 Criteria of Truth

Chapter Six: **Theories of Truth**

6.1 Principal Theories of Truth

6.2 The Correspondence Theory of Truth

6.3 Criticism of the Correspondence Theory of Truth

Chapter Seven: **The Coherence Theory of Truth**

7.1 Knowing What Coherence Theory Means

7.2 The Argument of Coherence Theory

7.3 Criticism of the Coherence Theory

Chapter Eight: **The Pragmatic Theory of Truth**

8.1 Knowing What Pragmatism Is

8.2 The Pragmatic Theory of Truth in Peirce

8.3 The Pragmatic Theory of Truth in James

8.4 The Pragmatic Theory of Truth in Dewey (Instrumentalism)

8.5 Criticism of the Pragmatic Theory of Truth

Chapter Nine: **Further Theories of Truth**

9.1 Supplementary Theories of Truth

9.2 Dialectical Theory of Truth

9.3 Pluralist Theory of Truth

9.4 Relativist Theory of Truth

9.5 Semantic Theory of Truth

9.6 Deflationist or Minimalist Theory of Truth

9.7 Consensus Theory of Truth

Part Three: Alternatives to Traditional Epistemology

Chapter Ten: **Indigenous Knowledge Systems and *Akonuche*.**

10.1 Epistemicide

10.2 Epistemological Decolonization

10.3 Indigenous Knowledge Systems

10.4 African Epistemology

10.5 *Akonuche* in Igbo Epistemology

Chapter Eleven: **Recent Topics in Epistemology**

11.1 Current Issues in Epistemology

11.2 Agnotology

11.3 Post-Truth Phenomenon

11.4 Artificial Intelligence

CONCLUSION

GLOSSARY

BIBLIOGRAPHY

FOREWORD

An ancient Greek philosopher, Plato, made a significant theoretical contribution to the understanding of knowledge. He delineated the differences between knowledge (*episteme*), belief (*pistis*), and opinion (*doxa*), enlightening us on the complexities of human understanding. Since then, philosophers have rigorously examined the multifaceted nature of human knowledge, leaving no aspect unquestioned. Epistemology, as a result, has emerged as the theoretical inquiry and study of human knowledge.

With the benefit of hindsight, from Plato's *Theaetetus* (c.400BC) down to Immanuel Kant's *Critique of Pure Reason* (1781) and the writings of contemporary philosophers, epistemologists have shown greater interest in propositional knowledge (knowing that) than other aspects viz. (Knowing how) and knowledge by acquaintance. This preferential favor for propositional knowledge is because it can yield to justification, truth, and belief, implying that the three components can individually and collectively serve as the necessary and sufficient conditions for achieving knowledge.

This standard analysis, often referred to as the reigning doctrine for centuries, was significantly challenged when Edmund Gettier published a concise two-page article titled "Is Justified True Belief Knowledge?" in 1963. The appearance of this paper in print marked a significant departure from the historical tradition, with some epistemologists rising against Gettier, accusing him of dismantling an ancient 'thought' akin to the ancient belief in Ptolemaic Science. But what was his offense? Through his essay, Gettier attempted to show that there are instances of justified true belief that cannot be regarded as cases of knowledge, and, therefore, the standard definition of knowledge is inadequate as it is not immune to error. Despite a welter of responses to Gettier's type-examples by some philosophers like Keith Leher, Ernest Sosa, Thomas Paxion, and Jonathan Dancy, amongst others, the challenge to the traditional definition by Gettier remains inconclusive, keeping the discourse alive and engaging.

A rich array of topics in epistemology may not all be treated in a single book. It must have prompted the author, Dr. Humphrey Ani, a Catholic Priest, to discuss randomly selected topics, bearing in mind their interconnectedness and alignment with the book's overall goal. Still in keeping with the objective of the book- to show that knowledge is not an exclusive property or inheritance of any people or race as was erroneously held during the colonial experience when the likes of Lucien Levy-Bruhl (1857-1939) denied Africans the capacity for rational thinking in his fangled bricolage "logical v. pre-logical mentalities." Some scholars have shown how Levy-Bruhl's proposition was faulty as it was an insult against the Black race. This is the perspective of the Portuguese sociologist Boaventura de Sousa Santos, who was reputed to have coined "Epistemicide in epistemology," which refers to the destruction or devaluation of indigenous knowledge systems by dominant epistemologies. For Sousa Santos and the chorus of other scholars, like Linda Alcoff and Linda Smith, amongst others, whose writings are directed toward reviewing monolithic European epistemology, epistemological decolonization is a task that must be accompanied.

The book is divided into three main parts, with parts one and two dealing with issues in mainstream epistemology and part three focusing primarily on the indigenous knowledge systems. One striking feature of this section is the introduction within the discourse of African epistemology, such Igbo notions as *amanife, akonuche, nkweye*, etc., which the author creatively and hermeneutically treated as paralleling the English terms like knowledge, mind, intelligence, belief, respectively. The idea here is that these Igbo concepts share a 'family resemblance ', a concept in Wittgensteinian philosophy that suggests that members of a family may not all share a single characteristic, but they share enough characteristics to be considered part of the same family, with epistemological notions elsewhere.

The author also devoted space for the treatment of Artificial Intelligence (AI), now designated as the Fourth Industrial Revolution (4IR or 4.0), which, I believe, will interest most students of Philosophy in their already familiar terrain of philosophy of mind, cognitive science, empiricism, etc. Their critical and analytical interrogation will expose the ethical implications of AI, particularly its generative aspect, which raises questions about the ethical use of AI and its potential impact on society. The book will be a valuable resource for students in tertiary institutions, the general public, and policymakers desiring to deepen their critical thinking skills and resonance in practice and public affairs.

Amaechi Udefi
Professor of Philosophy
University of Ibadan

and

Visiting Scholar,
University of Ghana,
June 2024.

INTRODUCTION

Conventionally, human knowledge has been defined by many epistemologists as "justified true belief." However, the entailment of this definition has raised further debates and questions, and its thesis remains a cause for many problems in epistemology. The disparate details that constitute the nature of the three principal terms in this definition: "belief," "justification," and "truth" have become the basis of vast epistemic problems in defining and explaining the nature and meaning of human knowledge. The questions that arise from this, such as the meaning of belief in the context of human knowledge, the implications when justification is not justified, and the identification of truth in what we claim to know, are not just academic exercises, but they are crucial for our understanding of the world. They engage us in a profound intellectual journey. Are there alternatives to defining and explaining human knowledge? And are there emerging problems affecting knowledge as a human act in the new world order? Responding to these questions and reflecting on these issues are the main objectives of this work.

Part One of this work will comprehensively explore the meaning of human knowledge, from etymology to its problems and their implications. Discussions in this segment will form chapters One and Two of the work.

Chapter One will delve into the etymology and nature of human knowledge as consciousness, providing a comprehensive understanding. It will further explain human knowledge theoretically, leaving no aspect untouched.

Chapter Two will raise questions on what generally constitutes the problems of human knowledge in epistemology, providing a comprehensive view of the issues. It will reflect on the perspectives that created the problems and their implications in what we know and how we know, ensuring a comprehensive exploration of the topic.

Part Two will start from Chapters Three to Nine. It will look at the core elements of the definition of knowledge as justified true belief and explore the schools of thought and arguments associated with them, as well as the theories and criticisms related to their positions.

Chapter Three will begin by analyzing the three principal concepts that define human knowledge: Belief, justification, and truth. The meaning, the types, and the schools involved in explaining *belief* as a necessary element of human knowledge will be explored. Further discussion in this regard, with particular attention to *justification* of its associated problems as demonstrated by Bertrand Russell and Edmund Gettier in his *Gettier problem*, will continue in Chapter Four.

Chapters Five, Six, Seven, Eight, and Nine will contain detailed reflections and criticisms on the term, theories, and problems of *truth* as a significant mark of the definition of human knowledge.

Part Three of the work will address the problems emanating from the monolithic epistemological methodology created by occidental scholarship tradition. In an effort to decolonize the study of human knowledge, it will comment on contemporary alternatives to traditional epistemology.

Chapter Ten in this segment will examine the new alternative methodologies of epistemology as seen in Indigenous Knowledge Systems, using African epistemology as a case study. The concept of *Akonuche* and its morphological analysis in Igbo epistemology will be introduced as a new epistemic and heuristic proposition.

In Chapter Eleven, the concluding chapter of the work, emerging issues in epistemology will be introduced and briefly discussed. This chapter will engage contemporary issues in epistemology, like agnotology, post-truth phenomena, and artificial intelligence, and examine their epistemological impacts in a hyperglobalized era like ours.

The conclusion will reflect the author's findings and position, sequel to the entire discussion of the work, thereby providing the audience with a sense of enlightenment and understanding.

PART ONE: HUMAN KNOWLEDGE

Chapter One: The Meaning of Human Knowledge

1.1 Etymology of Human Knowledge

Human knowledge is so evident and essential to human life that you cannot ignore it in the life of men and women. Everyone knows that we know, or things are known, but finding a clear and acceptable definition of knowledge is very demanding in epistemology. There have been a lot of debates and irreconcilable positions in defining knowledge, such as the debate between foundationalism and coherentism. Sometimes, definitions of knowledge by scholars have ended up in the explanations of its characteristics, descriptions of its processes, or enumerations of its forms. But these are also within the circumference of its definition and meaning.

The etymology of knowledge could be seen in the Latin *gnoscere* or the Greek *gignoskein,* which relates to the Old English *gecnāwan,* meaning "to recognize," "to identify," "to know," "to perceive." The current English word "knowledge" connotes various states distinguished in other modern languages. The verb "to know" can be translated into French either as *"connaitre"* or as *"savoir,"* and the noun "knowledge" can be translated into Latin as either *"cognitio"* or as *"scientia."* Connotations of knowledge in the English language include consciousness, comprehension, cognition, recognition, apprehension, understanding, awareness, realization, familiarity, insight, acquaintance, etc. These connotations, therefore, make its etymology and lexicology complicated. This is why a lexicological study might not be enough to understand the various nuances of the meaning of knowledge.

1.2 Knowledge as Consciousness

From the various root studies and connotations of the word, knowledge simply and essentially means awareness or consciousness. This awareness involves familiarity or understanding of someone or something, like facts, information, descriptions, skills, systems, reasons/propositions, etc. When we say we know something, we mean that we are aware or conscious of that thing. This is why Joseph Omoregbe writes that:

> Knowledge presupposes consciousness. All thinking, all acquisition of knowledge, and even skepticism itself presupposes consciousness. Thus, consciousness is basic to epistemology and is the veritable starting point of any discussion about knowledge. For, it is because man has consciousness (reflective consciousness) that he can acquire knowledge, can justify his knowledge or can even doubt.[1]

Consciousness is the awareness of our experience in which a subject internally and intentionally becomes aware of an object outside of himself or within himself. As I wrote in *Critical History According to Bernard Lonergan*, "Consciousness has to do with the mind's self-possession in an ontological manner, which could happen at the sensitive or intellective level. Consciousness is all about the awareness in the mind, of the external or internal experiences of the subject."[2] It is essentially an activity of

---

[1] Joseph Omoregbe, *Epistemology (Theory of Knowledge), A Systematic and Historical Study* (Lagos: Joja Press Limited, 1998),1.
[2] Humphrey Uchenna Ani, *Critical History According to Bernard Lonergan* (Rome: Gregorian and Biblical Press, 2017), 249.

the mind, that is, something that happens within the human mind, and as such, it is personal to the individual. It is not a collective or group act, and it does not happen outside the mind, even though its object could be outside the mind.

The known object, which is the object of consciousness is located outside the mind, whether it is the consciousness of an *external object* (objective external experiences) or *an internal object* (subjective internal experiences). The former may refer to external physical environment like objects of sense perceptions, while the latter may refer to internal environments like awareness of thoughts, feelings, and behaviors. Consciousness or knowledge is the activity of the mind when one is aware that he or she thinks, believes, imagines, sees, listens, feels, deliberates, etc.

Given that consciousness happens internally in the subject, its content is not accessible to any other person outside the subject. This is why no one can really know what I think, what I imagine, what I see, etc., unless I tell someone. Without my telling someone what I have in mind, no one can access what I am conscious of.[3] As the content of my consciousness is strictly personal and private to me, I may decide not to tell anyone what it really is, thereby telling a lie. In the acts of consciousness, everyone is the master of his or her mind's content. As Omoregbe puts it: "The fact that a man's subjectivity, his innermost being, is inaccessible to any other man "is a reflection" of the dignity of the human person. Everyman is the sole master of his own subjectivity; he alone has access to it and can know what is in it."[4]

---

[3] Cf. Omoregbe, *Epistemology*, 2.
[4] Omoregbe, *Epistemology*, 3.

Again, given that the act of consciousness is very real and immanent in me, it is indubitable. I cannot doubt what I am conscious of. It is so indubitable in me that to doubt what I am conscious of will be tantamount to self-contradiction.[5] And consciousness being a subjective act does not happen in space too. It is an intentional operation of the mind, which is not spatial, physical, quantified, or localized. When I think for instance, my thinking is within me and not located or localized in any exterior space. Nevertheless, it takes place in time. As Omoregbe writes: "when I am thinking about something, I am doing so at a particular time but not in any space."[6]

Consciousness is also continuous in that it is always at work except when asleep, comatose, or dead. For as long as one remains conscious, one's mind is always in operation, moving from one object of awareness to another, seeing, thinking, imagining, questioning etc. When one is unable to do this, we can say that he or she has lost his or her consciousness, or that he or she is unconscious like when one is comatose or dead.

Consciousness is reflexive. If I am conscious of something, I am not just only conscious of that thing. I am also conscious of my consciousness of that thing. It is essential to understand that animals lacking *reflexive* consciousness are not conscious of their consciousness. This is part of why they cannot question the objects of their awareness. This limitation in animals, which we humans do not share with them, gives us a perspective on the unique nature of human consciousness. Animals do not engage in creative and reflexive functions about their consciousness.

---

[5] Cf. Omoregbe, *Epistemology*, 2.
[6] Omoregbe, *Epistemology*, 3.

Omoregbe remarks, "Not only does man know, but he also knows that he knows. Not only is he conscious, but he is also conscious of his consciousness."[7]

This relates to the fact that consciousness can have the *internal experiences* of the subject knower as its object. One can be conscious of oneself. Such epistemic awareness is called self-consciousness. In *Critical History*, I described it as "one's awareness of the things immanent or interior to the subject." [8] Reflexivity of consciousness (or self-consciousness) is the first indicator and sign that defines man differently from other brutes by raising him from instincts to intellect. Man is essentially a conscious being. Man exists and finds meaning in his existence because he is conscious and knows that he is conscious. One recalls here that René Descartes in his *Second Meditation* has defined man as "a conscious being (*res cogitans*) ...a being [that] doubts, understands, asserts, denies, is willing, is unwilling; further, that has sense and imagination."[9]

Many human acts like sensing, desiring, wishing, and making choices are rooted in his consciousness as a being that knows. Ben Okwu Eboh in this regard, observes that various acts of humans through which we share in the structures, the forces, and the energies of the space-temporal universe-, ourself being part of the structure, are but germination and prolongation of our consciousness or knowledge.[10] Hence, Ugo Viglino remarks that mankind is

---

[7] Omoregbe, *Epistemology*, 4.
[8] Ani, *Critical History*, 249.
[9] Rene Descartes, "Meditations on First Philosophy," in *Descartes Philosophical Writings*, trans. and ed. E. Anscombe and P.T. Geach (London: Nelson's University Paperbacks, 1975), 70.
[10] Cf. Ben Okwu Eboh, *Basic Issues in the Theory of Knowledge* (Nsukka: Fulladu Publishing Company, 1995),109.

constituted, conserved, and continued in the material order of the universe because of his consciousness.[11]

Everything has meaning for mankind because it is given in our consciousness or knowledge. We make meaning of our existence depending on the measure and the way we know. Thus, the absence of knowledge is the absence of human reality, and definitive suspension of knowledge is absolute absence of man.[12] In corroborating this, Eboh writes that: "In fact, all that man does not in any way know, all that stands totally outside the rays of his apprehension, experience and sensation, all that he cannot imagine, suspect, desire, fear, is for him as if it did not exist."[13] Therefore, man is all that he is and does, and values in the measure and to the extent he knows. Consciousness defines the essence and existence of man. The power in man is his knowledge, or put in the Baconian dictum, "knowledge is power."[14]

It is knowledge that gives man the mastery position in the order of the universe. The uniqueness of man and the highness of man as part of the universe are because of his intelligence, self-awareness, and self-consciousness. That man is aware of himself is a height which no other created being in the universe has been able to attain. Eboh writes that:

> We can, in fact, say that man is the presence of the world to itself because despite the immensity, [the] power, and

---

[11] Cf. Ugo Viglino, *La Conoscenza* (Roma: Pontificia Universitas Urbaniana, 1969), 50.
[12] Cf. Viglino, *La Conoscenza*, 70.
[13] Eboh, *Theory of Knowledge*, 110.
[14] Francis Bacon, *The Works of Bacon, Vol XIV* eds. James Spedding, Robert Leslie Ellis, and Douglas Denon Heath (Boston: Brown and Taggard, 1861), 95.

the mystery of the universe, it would remain in a metaphysical coma if there were no man to give it a name. Man is, in a way, the 'world' through which the world speaks. The World, as it were, is helpless without man. It cannot speak to itself; it cannot know itself.[15]

Man defines and recreates the world by his intelligence and has continued to shape and re-shape the created universe by the same faculty. Thus, Theilhard de Chardin describing this great leap of man, in his reflection on human evolution writes:

> Once life, along this ray, reached a critical point of arrangement…it became hypercentred upon itself to the point of becoming capable of foresight and invention. It became conscious 'in the second degree.' And this was sufficient to enable it in a few hundreds of thousands of years to transform the surface and appearance of the earth.[16]

In the second stage of the human evolution according to de Chardin, human life experienced "an explosion of consciousness," and this birth of consciousness or knowledge changed everything about human life. It gave humankind power to know, control, recreate, re-invent, and transform the surface and the appearance of the universe with creativity, foresight, discovery, innovations, and inventions. From that moment in the life of humankind, knowledge has continued to grow and expand, emanating from various dimensions of human existentiality. Knowledge can emanate from perception, experience,

---

[15] Eboh, *Theory of Knowledge*, 108.
[16] Theilhard de Chardin, *Man's Place in Nature* (London: Fontana/Collins Press, 1974), 62.

thinking, reasoning, inquiry, discovery, intuition, education, or many other ways.

There are different forms of knowledge as consciousness. In certain forms, one may be clearly aware that one knows, and we can say that such knowledge is explicit, and one is therefore clearly conscious of one's act of knowing. In other cases, one may not be clearly conscious in one's act of knowing, thus, one's knowledge or consciousness would be tacit. In this case, one may be said to lack explicit consciousness or self-consciousness as a knower.

There can also be knowledge as consciousness of individuals or things that might be different from facts about them. There can also be knowledge of how things are done as different from real constituents, nature, and information of those things. These forms of knowledge explain why there could be a difference between knowing that something is the case and knowing how to handle something. Details of these dimensions of knowledge constitute the theoretical meaning and explanations of the term: *Knowledge*, beyond its etymology and lexicology.

1.3 Theoretical Explanation of Knowledge

Beyond the etymological explanation, theoretical definition of knowledge is always ambiguous. The ambiguity in defining knowledge was captured by C.N. Bittle when he writes that "just because it is a primary act of experience, the idea of knowledge eludes every effort at an exact definition."[17] The reason for this is because there are many

---

[17] C.N. Bittle, *Reality and the Mind* (New York: The Bruce Publishing Company, 1936), 12.

ways one can claim to know something. To avoid the ambiguity of theoretical definition therefore, it might be advisable to apply ostensive definition of knowledge in our case here.[18] In this way, we shall be looking at the definition of knowledge from its instances and characteristics. Thus, Russell in his works, *On Denoting* and *Problems of Philosophy,* defined knowledge by positing two ways or instances of knowledge. According to him, there is knowledge by *acquaintance* and knowledge by *description*.[19]

In knowledge by acquaintance, he explains that a person is acquainted with an object when he stands in a "direct cognitive relation to the object, *i.e.* when (the subject is) directly aware of the object itself."[20] According to him, "we have *acquaintance* with anything of which we are directly aware, without the intermediary of any process of inference or any knowledge of truths."[21] Knowledge by acquaintance gives the subject immediate or unmediated awareness of some propositional truth. Thus, one acquires knowledge by virtue of causal connection or contact that he or she has with other persons, objects, and locations that are presented to him or her.

---

[18] In theoretical definition, there is formulation of adequate scientific nature and characters of the description and meaning for which a term applies. In ostensive definition, a term is defined by pointing at its instances in order to express its meaning. Its examples express the term and its meaning. Cf. Francis Offor, *Essentials of Logic* (Ibadan: Book Wright Publishers, 2014), 59.
[19] Cf. Bertrand Russell "On Denoting," in *Mind* 14, no. 56 (1905): 479-480.
[20] Bertrand Russell, "Knowledge by Acquaintance and Knowledge by Description," in *Proceedings of the Aristotelian Society* 11, (1910): 108.
[21] Bertrand Russell, *Problems of Philosophy*, ed. John Perry (Oxford: Oxford University Press, 1912), 46.

Knowledge by acquaintance can be pure or impure. In pure knowledge by acquaintance, there is often no doubt entertained because the subject and the object of knowledge are more directly involved or united. But where there is impure acquaintance, like the case of a sick person trying to figure out or explain his real places or sources of pain, there may be doubt or uncertainty. In this case, there may be a need to demand more evidence for assurance and acceptance.

In knowledge by description, one knows something by encountering their descriptions through verbal descriptions, images, writings, paintings, and other media of description available to one in relation to the object of description. Knowledge by description is not only propositional in nature but inferential, mediated, or indirect. Given that it involves a medium of explanation, descriptive knowledge cannot be accepted with zero doubt. Some elements of doubt might arise, and additional evidence might be needed to assure its certainty and acceptance.

In a related reflection, Eboh explains in his *Theory of Knowledge*, that one can know something by familiarity or acquaintance, experience, or through a technical mastery of something.[22] I can say that I know Bettolino in Milan because I have been there and lived there too. That is knowledge by acquaintance or familiarity. Here, there is a direct awareness and familiarity by the subject of knowledge (me) with the object of knowledge (Bettolino). The knower and the known are united through a direct familiarity. The familiarity or acquaintance may be sufficient for one's claim to know something in this way of knowing, without seeking additional information or

---

[22] Cf. Eboh, *Theory of Knowledge*, 6.

justification for such knowledge claim. This is slightly like, but different from when I say: I know what hunger is. In this latter case, I know of hunger because I have experienced hunger. It is knowledge by experience, and my experience of hunger is sufficient for my claim of knowledge of hunger.

But if I say that I know how to ride a bicycle, it is another kind of knowledge which is neither based on familiarity nor experience but on having skill in a system or an art. Such knowledge is more of skillful ability than of experience or acquaintance. It is "know-how" kind of knowledge, where knowledge would mean mastering of something.[23] As Keith Lehrer would put it, it is knowledge by a "special form of competence."[24] Michael Polanyi in his *Personal Knowledge* on the nature of knowledge by its forms, argues that there is a clear difference between *knowledge how* and *knowledge that*.[25] He used the example of the knowledge of the theory of the balance involved in riding a bicycle and the skill of riding a bicycle to demonstrate this. Of course, both are forms of knowledge about bicycle riding. The difference is that knowing the law of physics involved in maintaining balance-in-riding is theoretical; but knowing the skill of riding and being able to ride the bicycle is practical. The theoretical knowledge in

---

[23] Cf. Eboh, *Theory of Knowledge*, 6.
[24] Keith Lehrer, *Knowledge* (Oxford: Clarendon Press, 1974), 1.
[25] Cf. Michael Polanyi, "Tacit Knowing: Its Bearing on Some Problems of Philosophy," in *Reviews of Modern Physics*, 34 (4) Oct. 1962, 601-616,
http://www.compilerpress.ca/Competitiveness/Anno/Anno%20Polanyi%20Tacit%20Knowlng%20RMP%201962.

this example is *knowledge that*, while the practical dimension is *knowledge-how*.

Gilbert Ryle equally discussed this, acknowledging the difference between *knowing-how* to do something and *knowing-that* a proposition is true or false.[26] The former refers to practical knowledge, while the latter refers to propositional knowledge.[27] He writes that Philosophers have not done justice to this distinction which is quite familiar to all of us between knowing that something is the case and knowing how to do things. He argues that in their theories of knowledge, philosophers often concentrate on the discovery of truths or facts, and most times, they either ignore the discovery of ways and methods of doing things or else they try to reduce it to the discovery of facts. They often assume that intelligence equates with the contemplation of propositions and are exhausted in this contemplation.[28] Thus, he adds that failure to acknowledge this distinction can only lead to infinite regress in epistemology.[29]

In propositional knowledge therefore, unlike in practical knowledge, there is a declarative statement which carries a truth-value. That is, there is factual expression, which can be true or false (truth value). Most often, the more

---

[26] Cf. Gilbert Ryle, "Knowing How and Knowing That-The Presidential Address," in *Meeting of the Aristotelian Society at the University of London Club on November 5th, 1945, at 8, pm.* Preamble, https://academic.oup.com/aristotelian/article-abstract/46/1/1/1805552?redirectedFrom=fulltext&login=false

[27] Cf. *The Stanford Encyclopedia of Philosophy, Supplement to Gilbert Ryle, Some Problems in Contemporary Work on Knowing-How and Knowing*-accessed July 2023, https://plato.stanford.edu/entries/ryle/knowing-how.html

[28] Cf. Ryle, "Knowing How and Knowing That," Preamble.

[29] Cf. Jason Stanley and Timothy Williamson, "Knowing How," *Journal of Philosophy*, 98(8): 411–444, 2001.

critical questions, debates and arguments in epistemology revolve around propositional knowledge because of the efforts to challenge, justify and defend its truth value. The same may not apply in practical or procedural knowledge where the emphasis is on acquisition of skill and method (in knowing-how things function or operate).

We can deduce then that knowledge can be propositional (where truth of facts and logic are understood), procedural (where skill of performance is acquired), and by acquaintance (where objects, events, places, or persons are perceived/encountered or experienced). In simpler expression, I can say that I *know that* 1+1=2 (theoretical), and that I *know how* to add 1+1 to get 2 (practical), and that I *know* 2 villages in Egede town (acquaintance).

It is important to note, unlike in English language, that the distinctions in the nuances of meaning of knowledge are reflected in the way the word, is understood in some other modern European languages like French, Portuguese, Spanish, German, Dutch and Italian. Italians make a distinction between knowledge as *sapere* and knowledge as *conoscere*. The former is theoretical and descriptive while the latter involves acquaintance or personal experience. In similar epistemology, the Germans have *kenne* and *wissen*, the Spanish have *saber* and *conocer*, while the French have *savoir* and *connaitre*. In some non-Western epistemologies like African epistemology, the distinctions, and non-distinctions of the terms for knowledge, may depend on their contextual and cultural applications.

However, the etymological and theoretical explanations of knowledge constitute an initial part of understanding human knowledge. The main task lies in explaining the epistemological meaning of human knowledge. There have been various arguments, debates, theories, ideas, speculations, demonstrations, and explanations of the meaning of human knowledge in epistemology. In the history of epistemology, many definitions of human knowledge have been faulted or falsified, while others have been modified. There have also been assumptions often taken or mistaken to be human knowledge. There have also been assertions made or believed, with or without verification, and seen as human knowledge. It is this explosion of definitions, speculations, conceptualizations, and theorizations that have created epistemological problems of knowledge. Engaging these problems demands deeper inquiries of what constitutes the questions on it. It will require an expanded harvest of the perspectives that have been articulated in addressing the problems in the course of history of epistemology, as well as the implications evolving from them.

Certainly, discussions on the problems of human knowledge will open wider reflections on the entailment, the arguments, and the theories of the principal terms that define human knowledge, which include *belief*, *justification*, and *truth*. Discussing problems of knowledge, especially in our time will certainly draw attention to non-traditional topics or recent themes in epistemology like Indigenous Knowledge Systems, African epistemology, *akonuche* in Igbo epistemology, agnotology, artificial intelligence etc.

Chapter Two: **The Problems of Human Knowledge**

2.1 What Constitutes the Problems of Human Knowledge?

I participated in a conversation with a friend who wants to let me *know* who a witch is. He told me that a witch is a feminine creature or woman who is believed to have malignant magical powers and who flies in the dark to carry out evil operations.[30] I asked about how he arrived at such a creature, and he responded that he heard about it from people, and that he has seen those believed to be victims of the operations of the witch. I further asked if he knew how the witch flies, that is, if the witch uses a sort of invisible propeller that pushes it into the air space or flies with the wings. In answer to this, he said that the witch can fly on wings sometimes, in that case it is a winged creature. In some cases, it can fly on a broom which propels it into the sky.

Meanwhile, he alluded that a witch is a normal living person in a community, who transmogrifies her anatomical structures and exercises a metaphysical potentiality that enables her to execute powers that are extra-human like flying and hurting people. I listened to him attentively for the rest of his details on the nature, operations and even the spiritual forces that can attract witchcraft as well as the prayers for repelling them.

---

[30] There is no intention for denigration of the female sex/feminine gender here. The identification of witch here as a *feminine creature* or *woman* is because the term is feminine, with its masculine equivalence as wizard.

After the narrative, I had to engage my friend as an epistemologist. I asked of why he believed what he was told about a witch even though he has never seen one. He answered that he had seen the evil impact of those attacked by a witch. I asked if he has evidence to prove or justify that the physical impact, he saw on the people he believed to be victims of the witch are true. He responded that people, including the victims testified to that. I asked if he, himself had ever been a witch victim, and he responded no. I asked if he has ever seen a witch flying on the broom in the dark or winged witch in operation, and he responded on the negative.

His belief about a witch was based on testimony of the people. His reason was based on rational imagination that such a creature is possible since it is possible to rationally imagine a female person possessing flying capacity with which it can foment or operate evil. His belief had no direct empirical justification. The only indirect empirical evidence he could allude was the claim of having seen victims of the witch. But he could not provide sufficient evidence to substantiate that a witch hurt the acclaimed victim, or that the physical effect on the said victim is an act or craft of a witch.

How then does one accept knowledge of a witch on these epistemic loopholes? Is my friend's knowledge of a witch dependable? What type of knowledge has he about a witch? On what ground will one be persuaded to accept what he claims to know about a witch? Could one accept his knowledge of a witch based on his experience or acquaintance with a witch? Is his acceptance of the proposition that there is a witch demonstrable or provable by any logic or skill? And is it enough to accept his belief that there exists a witch based on the testimony he got from people, especially in the absence of demonstrable evidence over what he avowed as the physical effect of a witch? Does his believing that there is a witch, sufficiently, justify that he knows that there is a witch? How true is his knowledge of a witch even if he believes that? Is it also possible that he believes what is not true? How if his knowledge is at best a belief based on fictional imagination, supported only by popular testimony which could be false? Is his belief in a witch reasonably defendable? Raising questions of this kind over anything one claims to believe or know begins the problem of knowledge in epistemology.

When we talk of the problems of knowledge in epistemology, we are talking about questions raised over what we claim to know and how we do know what we know. The problems about knowledge ask questions on how to set up the criteria for the justification of what we know. This is why the problems of knowledge are tantamount to the questions of reasons for knowledge. How do I know that what I know is true? How do I know what I know, and what I do not know? What evidence can make what I claim to know to be true? If a witch exists, does that imply that it is true that I know of a witch and that I know that it exists, or rather that it is true that it exists? And if I do not believe that there is a witch, does that also cancel the possibility that a witch exists, truly? Thus, the problems of knowledge revolve around the nature of knowledge, the method of knowledge, the sources of knowledge, the certainty or doubts on knowledge and the mental attitude of acceptance (belief) or rejection of knowledge (doubt).

The problems of knowledge in epistemology are highly debatable and complex. They spur challenging philosophical queries and questions on knowledge. Is knowledge mere awareness? Do we always understand what we know? How do we recognize what is true knowledge? Is what I know based on what I perceive or on how I perceive it? How do I come to know what I know, if truly I know it? How do I know and accept what I know to be true? Is what I believe the same as what I know to be true? Interrogations of this kind are precisely the reasons why Plato cautioned and recommended that we must be able to make a distinction between knowledge and belief, and that we must be able to identify true knowledge as different from opinion. In the effort to find the various dimensions of the problems of knowledge, various perspectives have arisen in the critical study of human knowledge otherwise termed epistemology.

2.2 Perspectives on the Problems of Human Knowledge

The problems of understanding and the meaning of knowledge have led to many schools and perspectives in epistemology. The principal perspectives making the problems of knowledge include idealism, realism, skepticism, foundationalism, empiricism, rationalism, externalism, and internalism. These perspectives exist as *part of, not apart* from the main epistemological discussions and debates on answering questions and doubts raised on the nature and justification of human knowledge.

Idealism is the thesis of some philosophers who claim that it is the human mind that shapes and decides knowledge of the existing external reality. In that case, realities cannot exist or be known to exist outside the mind of the subject who knows. All that we know become real or true only by the ability of the human mind which constructs or shapes the reality. Realities or objects exterior to us remain questionable for them, and as such are unknown until our minds recognize them. Of course, our minds do create knowledge out of necessity from the things around us, otherwise called objects of epistemic experience. Idealists agree that the human mind has the enormous potential for producing something out of nothing. The human mind, therefore, is the ultimate source of knowledge and as such a valid or an ideal reality. As I mentioned in my *Introduction to Epistemology*,

> Idealism as a system of epistemology holds that the object of knowledge is the product of mental operations. Knowledge for idealism subsists in ideas derived from the acts of the intellect of various modes. It agrees that there exists a mind-independent world, but all that can be known about it is dependent on the structures of the mind. Many idealists agree that most of what we know are acquired by *a priori* processes, or that knowledge is innate in man.[31]

The thesis of the idealists on what constitutes knowledge has been refuted and rejected by some other philosophers. These opponents have problems with reducing knowledge to only what the mind produces.

On the contrary, they posit that knowledge is based on the object perceived. They are called realists, and their argument is anchored on philosophical materialism which maintains that nothing in the material world emerges from the human mind. The material world or the external reality pre-exists before the mind and as such is independent of the mind. What the human mind does is to make effort to discover and know it. To do this, therefore, would require

---

[31] Humphrey Uchenna Ani, *Introduction to Epistemology* (Enugu: PUKKA Press, 2023), 186.

the use of the senses for feeling or the application of the human mind for intellection. According to Ani,

> Realism is a philosophical stance that natural things, known or perceived, exist independent of anyone thinking or perceiving them. It holds that there is a mind-independent reality existing in the world, which though can be perceived or conceived yet does not depend on perception or conception to be.[32]

A major and important problem in the study of human knowledge came from the perspectives of some philosophers who partially or entirely doubted the possibility or existence of human knowledge. They are called skeptics.

The central argument of sceptic philosophers is that what appears to be real may be false, and as such they raise doubts over every kind of knowledge. Some of them hold that what we call knowledge, either by the senses or the intellect, are actually mental constructs which do not reflect the real truth about what we claim to know. For them we must doubt everything since everything is uncertain. Sceptics question the possibility of knowledge. As Bittle writes: "Skepticism maintains that the mind cannot overcome doubt. For, the human reason is not only perverted and diseased, but it is in itself fallacious, weak, and unstable."[33] By their arguments, sceptics remind us that our knowledge can be fallible and weak in so many ways and by so many factors. Thus, we must be careful to avoid errors, mistakes, prejudices, and superstitions in the pursuit of true knowledge.[34] Sceptics believe that pluralities and

---

[32] Ani, *Introduction to Epistemology*, 185.
[33] Bittle, *Reality and the Mind*, 26.
[34] Cf. Ani, *Introduction to Epistemology*, 155.

polarities of perceptions make knowledge uncertain and constantly doubtful. This is why error persists in what we claim to know. Thus, Eboh writes that: "In our everyday experience, we witness that there are countless numbers of times that we fall into error at the level of sense knowledge and intellectual knowledge."[35] Error in knowledge makes it difficult to establish truth, and knowledge is not possible where truth is missing.

The first recorded sceptics in the history of philosophy were the Fifth Century Sophists, whose doubts over conventional customs and claims of knowledge gave birth to epistemology. There will be other sceptics after them down the history of philosophy, in virtually every epoch. Joseph Omoregbe in this light observes that:

> In fact, epistemology developed through the ages in Western Philosophy in response to the challenge of the sceptics. Thus, skepticism gives rise to the development of epistemology and in that sense, it has helped epistemology to grow. If I claim to know something with certainty and you say that certainty is impossible, I am challenged. I will try to prove to you that certainty is possible, that it is possible to know something with certainty. In other words, I will try to justify my claim to have certain knowledge. This is precisely what epistemologists have been doing.[36]

Opposed to skepticism are the perspectives of those who say that there are criteria for the possibility of knowledge. They maintain that there are epistemic foundations to believe in true knowledge. They represent a point of view termed foundationalism or dogmatism in

---

[35] Eboh, *Theory of Knowledge*, 17.
[36] Omoregbe, *Epistemology*, 8.

epistemology. The thesis of these philosophers according to Ani is that:

> Knowledge is possible and the certainty of it can be founded on or justified in an indisputable foundation or dogma. It upholds that there are propositions which we cannot fail to believe because they are true and cannot but be true in themselves. Foundationalism posits that certain basic beliefs are supposed to make up the foundation from which all other beliefs can be derived deductively or inductively. These beliefs are held to be evident or self-evident beyond dubitability, corrigibility and fallibility. Foundationalism is very much related to dogmatism, and their main streams of thought are so close that it is most times termed dogmatism by many scholars.[37]

Foundationalism argues that if certain kinds of knowledge cannot be contended, or cannot be proved, and do not need to be proven, and where we cannot even give reasons to support them, then, we are compelled therefore to believe them. This is because their truth naturally draws the ascent of the mind.[38] Alfred North Whitehead in this light argues that certain kind of knowledge like geometrical truth constitutes its own justification without needing any other justification to be true. He writes that if anyone says, "it seems to me that the whole is not greater than [any of] the parts, I will only tell him, 'Work out your own system'."[39] The aim of foundationalism or dogmatism as explained by Omoregbe is to,

---

[37] Ani, *Introduction to Epistemology*, 161.
[38] Cf. Ani, *Introduction to Epistemology*, 165.
[39] Alfred North Whitehead, *Essays in Science and Philosophy* (London: Rider and Cole, 1948), 138.

Erect an impregnable foundation of knowledge such that it would be immune to the criticism of critics. It is, in other words, an attempt to find an ultimate justification of knowledge, an ultimate principle of certainty that would guarantee the certainty of knowledge so that skeptics would not be able to find any loophole in it for criticism.[40]

And to achieve this aim, foundationalism applies certain epistemological methods to establish undisputable certainty of knowledge. Such methods include principles that do not need doubt or proof, faith in the faculties of understanding, and trust in authority and the power of intuition. They recognize for instance, that self-evident truths and sense data are basic and do not need justification or validation from other beliefs to be true.[41] However, though skepticism and foundationalism might have their reasons for their positions, their inability to take a unified stand on the possibility and uncertainty of human knowledge has left problems in epistemology.

There have also been problems among epistemologists in accepting where knowledge is derived from. Some claim that knowledge is derived from experience while others claim that knowledge is derived from reason. Those who claim that knowledge is a product of human experience are called empiricists while those who argue that knowledge arises from human reason are called rationalists. Empiricism as a perspective on the problems of knowledge posits that:

> The only way to knowledge is through experience...that all our knowledge comes only or primarily from sensory experience. It emphasizes that the sources of knowledge

---

[40] Omoregbe, *Epistemology*, 50.
[41] Cf. Ani, *Introduction to Epistemology*, 162.

are based on observation and perception. Sensory experience and evidence are the key factors in the acquisition of knowledge. It equally argues that traditions, customs, institutions, history, and many other sociological forms of knowledge are derived from the relations and interconnections of previous sense experiences.[42]

Empiricists argue that reason does not have inventive or creative meaning, that it is rather through human experience, using the senses and their activities that we can engage in inventive creativity. For them, it is through the experiences we gather from sensory things and activities that we can build scientific and technological knowledge. Every knowledge according to empiricism is derived from or is based on experience. Thus, true knowledge comes after (we have had) experience (*a posterior* knowledge).

It is through the experimentation, accumulation, manipulation, innovation, and management of object of sense experiences that knowledge is generated and processed for human survival and progress in a society. This school of thought holds that knowledge is the product of experience and statements on observations made via the senses. Even ideas that arise in the mind, equally need to be tested through experience in observable or factual realities. True and reliable knowledge for them is measured by its correspondence with facts and perceptible physical realities. Eboh writes that:

> The crucial point in empiricism is the idea that perception is at some point indubitable. It is free from the possibility of error because error has no place in what is given. Error is due to imagination or the frailty of human judgement. Because certain truths are given in experience, they

---
[42] Ani, *Introduction to Epistemology*, 177.

cannot be false; they are indubitable because they are in a sense necessarily true.[43]

Error in human knowledge according to empiricism is from the mind's operation as in judgement, not from the objects given in human experience. Thus, D.W. Hamlyn remarks that: "There is the assumption running through these discussions that error and uncertainty are due to the mind's own operations and there is in perception something given that is not in any way a product of the mind's operations and must therefore be free from error."[44]

Opposed to the empiricists are the rationalists who hold that reason is the major source and sustenance of knowledge. They appeal to reason as the main source of justification of human knowledge. According to them, the human mind can grasp certain truths contained in the various realities and activities of the human person and form the fountain from which we derive knowledge.

True and indubitable knowledge as seen in such areas of understanding as logic, ethics, mathematics, and metaphysics are derived by reasoning and not by experience. Thus, underlining the argument that true and reliable knowledge are products of the mind and not of bodily experiences. Knowledge for this school of thought comes prior to experience (*a priori* knowledge) and as such are inborn or innate. Therefore, even when certain elements of knowledge might need experiential facts, their truth and certainty are confirmed or justified by the innate structures and operations of the human mind (reason). This is why Eboh posits that "rationalists maintain that the only way to

---

[43] Eboh, *Theory of Knowledge*, 58.
[44] D.W. Hamlyn, *The Theory of Knowledge* (London: The Macmillan Press Ltd, 1977), 35.

true knowledge is reason which possesses innate ideas of all reality. Philosophy consists in the analysis of these innate ideas. This analysis is sufficient for the discovery of all truths. In effect, rationalists claim that all concrete knowledge comes from reason."[45] Hamlyn further adds that rationalists believe that "reason alone can prove that there are foundations for knowledge, and that even the senses require the guarantee that reason is supposed to provide."[46]

The problem of the sources of knowledge between experience and reason has raised further fundamental questions on the nature and study of human knowledge as Ani observes:

> In the attainment of human knowledge, is it what the mind contributes that is more important or what the mind receives through the senses from the environment, or are both equally important? Is thought more important than observation in cognition? Has the mind the power to discover truth by itself without the assistance of observation and experience? Can experience alone give knowledge without the interpretation of the mind?[47]

Attempts at resolving this problem between rationalism and empiricism in the modern age by the German philosopher, Immanuel Kant led to what today is called "Kantian mediation" in epistemology.[48] But even at that, the problem has persisted in the study of human knowledge.

The same problem of finding the true yardstick of human knowledge has equally led to the conflicts of comprehension over the ground for reliability of true

---

[45] Eboh, *Theory of Knowledge*, 56.
[46] Hamlyn, *The Theory of Knowledge*, 24.
[47] Ani, *Introduction to Epistemology*, 179.
[48] Cf. Ani, *Topics in Epistemology*, 60.

knowledge. Is it the authenticity of the knower that determines true knowledge or the authenticity of the object known? This question raises the problem of internalism and externalism in epistemology. Internalism argues that it is the mental state or experiences of the knower that constitute beliefs in knowledge. What a knower believes or accepts to be true must be what is accessible to him or her, and he or she decides its truth by his or her own perceptual experience and reasonable judgment. Rene Descartes and Bernard Lonergan are among the internalist philosophers who strongly argue that it is the authenticity of the subject that makes true knowledge. Internalism holds that,

> The truth of a belief which qualifies it as true knowledge rests with the subjective authenticity of the knower. The internal conditions of the subject like the saneness and rational rectitude or correctness of the knower are the reliable grounds for the justification of a belief and its acceptance as true knowledge.[49]

In opposition to the stance of the internalists are the externalists who argue that what makes a true knowledge depends on the external or empirical conditions outside the knower. They disagree with the internalist stance that it is experiential facts and logical judgments of the knower that determine what is true. John Locke and Alvin Goldman are among the epistemologists that subscribe to epistemic externalism as the reliable argument that explains the correct grounds for a belief to be true knowledge.[50]

Beyond the above key problems identified in the evaluation of human knowledge, there are other minimal

---

[49] Ani, *Introduction to Epistemology*,78.
[50] Cf. Stanford Encyclopedia of Philosophy. s.v. "The Analysis of Knowledge."

and similar problems associated with it. There are sometimes the problems of whether objects of knowledge are independent of the perceiver or the contrary (direct and indirect realism). Do objects of perception exist independent of the perceiver? Do what we know by perceptual cognition represent the truth of the object perceived? Or are our perceptions mere impressions or inferences? Do our psychological or physiological conditions intervene in knowing process or not? Could it be that we do not perceive the external world as it is, outside of our senses? Is there a perceptual intermediary that mediates between the perceiver and the object perceived like in a mirror?

So many thinkers have in most cases raised questions against various theories and thoughts on human knowledge thereby creating endless irreconcilable problems among epistemologists. Some, for instance, have raised questions against speculative knowledge that does not have pragmatic effects. What is the essence of knowledge, if it is not an instrument of solving human problems as John Dewey would ask. Phenomenalists and Idealists are at problems in their stances on what constitutes the object of human knowledge. Objectivism is yet to reconcile thoughts and theses with subjectivism on the sources of certainty and authenticity in the process and justification of human knowledge. Conventionalist thinkers and contextualist speculators have not resolved issues based on human knowledge, and so on and so forth.

2.3 Implications of Problems of Human Knowledge

Discussing the problems of knowledge already signals that there is no unified or acceptable notion of knowledge and what constitutes it. This may appear to put knowledge in a negative limelight, but the fact remains that exposing the problems associated with knowledge is what makes the term rich and dynamic in meaning. Evaluating the problems around the notion and nature of knowledge has been more contributive to the term. The crisis of knowledge contents has differentiated the term's understanding into special studies. There are today specializations and even schools of study on the meaning and forms of human knowledge. There are also many methods used in the study of human knowledge, from both the conventional or classical fields and the non-conventional ones as seen in the various approaches of Indigenous Knowledge Systems. The critical study of human knowledge as seen in the different perspectives shown above already indicates that the problems of knowledge create schools of epistemology like skepticism, foundationalism, rationalism, empiricism, contextualism etc.

Furthermore, the problems of knowledge have pushed some discussions to concentrate on special forms of knowledge and its details as specializations. Some disciplines of study have even avoided the lexical and notional debates and arguments of human knowledge and rather concentrated more on knowledge for professional and pragmatic productions. Specialists in creative and productive sciences like mathematics, physics, economics etc, are less interested in terminological meanings of knowledge. Their interest is essentially to specialize in the concrete forms of knowledge in various disciplines and to see how they can be used for pragmatic or productive ends.

Knowledge of Mathematics and Physics is used to build houses, bridges, roads etc. They are forms of knowledge based more on the practical than on the speculative. This does not rule out the fact that some speculative forms of knowledge engage in specializations that are also constructive of values of society and the individual persons like ethics and aesthetics. This diversity of purpose has directly or indirectly created specializations in what knowledge means to people and how it is applied or valued. It has led to a kind of sociology of knowledge in defining the purpose of knowledge and how it affects what people do professionally in the Sciences or the Humanities.[51] And university inclinations of exploring knowledge in different disciplines have generated what is today termed STEM courses and SOFT courses.[52]

Furthermore, a significant implication of problems of knowledge came from debates and arguments on sources of human knowledge. In the medieval age of philosophy,

---

[51] Cf. Chiara Succi, "Soft Skills for the Next Generation: Toward a Comparison between Employers and Graduate Students' Perceptions," *Sociologia del Lavoro*. 137: 244–256.

[52] STEM is an acronym for Science, Technology, Engineering, and Mathematics. These four fields of knowledge engage in knowing about the natural sciences, using what is known of them in innovation, technical problem-solving, and critical thinking. They are often known as hard skill knowledge, as different from soft skill knowledge. The SOFT skill courses on the other hand focus on knowledge of basic Humanity activities like intersubjectivity, psychology, axiology, character, communication, vocational relationship, teamwork, morality, philosophy, religion, and social problem solving. Cf. Robert E. Levasseur, "People Skills: Developing Soft Skills — a Change Management Perspective," *Interfaces*. (2013) 43 (6): 566–571. doi:10.1287/inte.2013.0703.

Augustine and Aquinas built on the theses of Plato and Aristotle to account for the origin of human knowledge. While Augustine argued that true knowledge emanates from divine light as illumination, Aquinas held that they are derived from the use of both the external and internal senses in the process of abstraction as Aristotle taught. Their divergent points of view appeared problematic on the epistemic unity of the sources of human knowledge.

In the modern era, the disparity, and polarities of perspectives between the rationalists and empiricists motivated Kant to deepen the notion of the process of knowing. He identified the significant roles of the *a priori* and *a posteriori* knowledge in understanding phenomenon or physical reality. In the same epoch, debates, and doubts over conventional truth saw some Enlightenment thinkers like Erasmus, Bacon and Voltaire question what constitutes the authority of knowledge. The debates and discussions by these thinkers led to a greater enlightened version of human understanding of science, spirituality, and society. Breakthroughs were wrought in science leading to the industrial revolution, and faith beliefs were cleansed of superstition with the brush of critical thinking and enlightenment.

In the contemporary era, the problems hanging on comprehension and interpretation of human knowledge have persisted. Logical and linguistic analysts have put in much effort to explain the meaning of human knowledge, especially where its definition has become problematic to draw a unified acceptance among scholars. The age long acceptable definition of human knowledge as *Justified True Belief* (JTB) was already and somehow getting criticisms in Bertrand Russell's 1948 book, *Human Knowledge: Its Scope and Limits*. And in 1963, the same definition of knowledge as JTB was challenged by Edmund Gettier's two-and-half paged article entitled: "Is Knowledge Justified True Belief?" This epistemic challenge opened several more problems on the definition and meaning of human knowledge which epistemologists have not been able to resolve till date. Arguments and debates emanating from ***the Gettier Problem*** as it is called, are at the heart of the problems of human knowledge in epistemology today. This emphasizes the fact that getting an accurate unified definition of knowledge is a big epistemic problem.

The *Gettier Problem* is a major implication on the problems associated with the definition of human knowledge. It profoundly spurred some professional epistemologists to realize their deep disagreement on what knowledge is or what it means to know. It raised pertinent questions on how the definition of knowledge has been examined or accepted in the history of epistemology. What are the implications of knowledge as justified true belief? What constitutes the cardinal definitional lexicons of human knowledge? What explanations have epistemologists offered in explaining the main tripartite technical terms on the definition of human knowledge: *Belief*, *Justification* and *Truth.*? What do these terms mean for epistemologists? What are the top thoughts and theories associated with the three terms in defining knowledge? What is belief? What is justification? What is Truth? And how do these three core concepts or elements relate to human knowledge?

PART TWO: CORE ELEMENTS OF HUMAN KNOWLEDGE

Chapter Three: Belief, Justification and Truth

3.1 Relationship of Knowledge to Belief, Justification and Truth

Some epistemologists have tried to identify the main characteristics of knowledge in which its meaning can still be obtained. Hamlyn in this light writes that, "One condition of being said to know something is that what one *claims* to know must *be the case*; if it is an object that one claims to know, this must *exist*, and if what one claims to know is formulable in a proposition, this *must be true*."[53] This subscribes properly to the idea that knowledge is characterized by the fact that something *must exist*, factually or logically (justification), it must be accepted (*claimed*) to exist (belief) and it must *be the case/true* (truth).

Thus, the three essential notions of knowledge include: that it must be justified, it must be true, and it must be believed. These elements must collectively constitute knowledge. The three must be involved because each will not satisfy the meaning of knowledge distinctly. Only justification cannot produce knowledge where belief and truth for instance are lacking. Truth alone cannot make knowledge where its justification and belief are missing.

---

[53] Hamlyn, *The Theory of Knowledge*, 79.

And only belief will not be able to form knowledge either, where justification and truth are absent. However, these terms are distinctly related to knowledge in one way or the other as we shall discuss further.

3.2 Knowledge and Belief

What is belief and how does it relate to knowledge? Belief is a key concept in religion and epistemology. But epistemology does not study belief in its religious sense. It rather studies belief in its relation to knowledge. In its epistemological sense therefore, knowing the meaning and difference between belief and knowledge is relevant in understanding when knowledge is accepted as true or false. Belief is important in the understanding of the notion of knowledge because it qualifies the status of one of the essential elements in the act of knowing, that is, the knowing subject. As Eboh remarks: "In the process of acquiring human knowledge, three essential elements enter into it, namely, the knowing subject, the known object and the mental act of knowing (cognition)."[54]

Belief constitutes the subjective state of the knower in the process of acquisition of knowledge. It is the attitude of the knower that something is the case, or that a proposition about the world is true or false. It is the stance of the knower in accepting or rejecting a proposition or an experience as true or not true. Belief is a significant condition for justification of knowledge as true or false. Hamlyn in this light writes that the conditions for knowledge will always include that: (a) "I believe it," (b) "I

---

[54] Eboh, *Theory of Knowledge*, 8.

had good ground on which to base the belief and, (c) the belief was true."[55]

Belief is an attitude that something or a proposition is the case or true.[56] It is an attitude about the world which can be either true or false.[57] To believe is to take something or a proposition to be true and to disbelieve something is to take something or a proposition to be false. Sometimes, belief is spontaneous and might not require introspection before acceptance. Believing that I will wake up tomorrow or that the sun will rise tomorrow might not require much introspection or reflection from me. This is why most beliefs are not occurrent, that is, requiring active attention in their form. They may just be dispositional, that is, having a mental disposition to accept that something is the case or not the case.[58]

The things we believe are those things we understand to be true, but which may not actually be true. This is why sometimes beliefs may not be objective. They are our voluntary or involuntary acts of acceptance or rejection of a position or proposition after our internal or personal standard of evidence or reason has been met. Subjective opinions, personal testimonies and anecdotal evidence can serve as believable materials even when they may lack epistemic veracity or objectivity. One can believe what one is convinced of, by one's personal standard of evidence, even when what he or she believes may not meet up with scientific or actual standard of evidence. In that case, one's belief is the necessary result of one's conviction

---

[55] Hamlyn, *The Theory of Knowledge*, 101.
[56] Cf. The Stanford Encyclopedia of Philosophy, s.v. "Belief."
[57] Cf. The Stanford Encyclopedia of Philosophy, s.v. "Belief."
[58] Cf. The Stanford Encyclopedia of Philosophy, s.v. "Belief."

and not that of actual or scientific evidence or logical reasonableness.

Sometimes, belief as firmly held opinion might not require justified information as required in human knowledge. It is more of psychological faith which might lack facts for its position. Belief is often rooted purely on personal conviction than personal experience. Most of what people believe may not be what they have experienced. People simply develop inner conviction over something which may not be inspired by intellectual or experiential evidence. This is why belief, even as an epistemic state of the mind, is very much related to faith as an article of religion. They are both anchored on inner conviction and not human intellect as such. And in most cases, even epistemic faith culminates in religious faith.

One can easily believe an epistemic opinion that is not verified or proved in facts or reason. In analogous way, one is more likely to believe articles of faith in religion without questioning and demanding verification in fact or justification in reason. A person who is skeptical over epistemological beliefs or accepted positions will not be less skeptical when faced with issues of belief in religious faith. On the contrary, a person who easily accepts beliefs of evidence and reason in epistemology is more disposed to accept beliefs of faith in religion.

Belief is related to human knowledge in many ways. In the first place, knowledge is a subset of belief because a *true belief* is actually what we call knowledge. Thus, knowledge is classically defined as ***justified true belief***. Knowledge is a fraction of belief that has satisfied the standard of evidence and reason to be accepted as true and objective. While belief refers to personal conviction, knowledge refers to the truth of facts and reasons justifying the belief. Knowledge is derived from a set of justified or true beliefs. Truth therefore becomes the necessary requirement for belief to become knowledge. It is such that if I say that I know something, what I claim to know can only be knowledge if I believe it, and if it is true. In that case, my belief will not be knowledge if it is not true.

My belief could be merely subjective opinion of something which is not knowledge because it lacks justification in fact or reason. It is the truth contained in what I believe in, that makes my belief in that thing knowledge. It further implies that truth measures the reliability and certainty of what we believe or know. If there is fullness of truth in what I know, it will be more reliable or certain than when there is partial or no content of truth. Thus, the full or partial content of truth in a belief is what defines its degree of certainty and reliability as knowledge.

In belief, the knower's mental attitude of acceptance or assent to a position or proposition may not be with full intellectual knowledge always, as to guarantee truth with certainty. Belief is more of an intellectual judgment with a feeling of acceptance, unlike disbelief, in which there is no sufficient ground for the justification of such judgement as true or not true. Belief is like a hanging truth, needing experiential or rational grounding for certainty as knowledge. Its acceptance as true varies in degrees and may depend on the evidence provided.

Therefore, levels of belief may come in the form of surmise, suspicion, or conviction. It may also vary according to its object of interest. This is why *belief in* someone, or something is different from *belief that* a statement or proposition is true or not. But in whichever degree or interest it might be expressed, belief becomes true only when the truth of a position or proposition becomes evident and is rationally sufficient for the knower who at such point becomes a believer.

The notion of belief in epistemology has occupied philosophers from ancient time of the Greeks. It was discussed by Socrates, Plato, and the Stoics in the context of differentiating it from truth or trust (*pistis*), opinion or acceptance (*doxa*), and position or stance of a philosopher (*dogma*). In Plato's *Theaetetus*, Socrates tried to see true knowledge as justified true belief (*episteme*) as different from dispositive belief (*doxa*).[59] In justified true belief, there are added reasonable and necessary plausible assertions, evidence, and proof to support a belief. But in a dispositive belief, there is a mere psychic state to accept or reject a proposition or a position. When one believes, one's attitude to what one regards to be true is justified to him or her. Thus, one's belief about anything or a person leads one to the acceptance of that thing. If one says: "I believe that coal is black," it means that one accepts the truth of a proposition that says: "coal is black."

At this point, it is also important to explain the semantic distinction between *belief in* and *belief that* in epistemology. Jonathan Dancy in his *A Companion to*

---

[59] It is important to note that the notion of knowledge as "justified true belief" though may be used to qualify the epistemic stance of some ancient philosophers, it is a concept that emerged in the Enlightenment age to counter knowledge as revealed true belief (revelation of God) as seen in the epistemology of many medieval philosophies like Augustine's illumination. However, knowledge as Justified True Belief has been popular among philosophers until the Twentieth century when it was challenged by Edmund Gettier and Alvin Goldman.

Epistemology holds that there is a clear distinction between *belief-that* and *belief-in*. In this regard, he writes:

> It is sometimes supposed that all beliefs are 'reducible' to propositional belief, belief-*that*. Thus, my believing you, might be thought a matter of any believing, perhaps, that what you say is true...It is doubtful, however, that non-propositional believing can, in every case, be reduced in this way. Debate on this point has tended to focus on an apparent distinction between belief-that and belief-in.[60]

Belief-that is often related to propositional attitude to a claim which can be either true or false. This is contrary to *belief-in* which relates to attitude to things or entities like trust or faith in a person. Sometimes *belief-in* may be associated with a person or a non-perceptible entity. Take for instance that one says: "Humphrey *believes that* what Max said is the case," whereby the statement expresses that Humphrey *believes that* the proposition said by Max is true (even if he does not trust Max as a person). His belief rests with the proposition (what Max said), and not in Max as a person. But if the statement says: "Humphrey *believes in* Max," it means more. It means that Humphrey *believes in* Max as a person who is trustworthy and he would likely accept whatever Max says based on such trust, and maybe with added evidence.

Furthermore, one can say: "I *believe that* 'we should love one another' as God commanded in the Bible." Here, "*believe*" is based on accepting the proposition of what God said in the Bible: "we should love one another." It might be different from when one says: "I *believe in* God." In this

---

[60] Jonathan Dancy, *A Companion to Epistemology,* trans. Jonathan Dancy and Ernest Sosa (Malden: Blackwell Publishers Ltd, 1997), 48.

case, there is an expression of trust and confidence in God, which goes beyond mere propositional attitude to personal trust. Believing in God (personal trust) might be the reason for believing that "we should love one another" (propositional attitude).

Thus, Dancy argues that: "if *belief-in* presupposes *belief-that*, it might be thought that the evidential standards for the former must be at least as high as standards of the latter. And any additional pro-attitude might be thought to require a further layer of justification not required for cases of *belief-that*."[61] This implies that *belief-in* involves a combination of propositional belief together with some further attitude (personal trust).[62] Some have used this same semantic distinction, even inversely, to argue that a propositional acceptance (*belief-that*) can lead to personal acceptance (*belief-in*). Thus, a *belief that* God exists may become a necessary pre-condition for a *belief in* God.[63]

3.3 Types of Belief

There are also diverse types of belief. Epistemologists have categorized belief based on their ontological status, degree, object, or semantic properties. Belief can be occurrent or dispositional. It is occurrent when one is actively conscious of the representation associated with the object of belief. In this case, there is a more conscious involvement in what one believes in, that is, what one accepts or rejects as true or false. Belief can also be dispositional when the

---

[61] Dancy, *A Companion to Epistemology*, 49.
[62] Cf. Dancy, *A Companion to Epistemology*, 49.
[63] Cf. John N. Williams, "Belief-in and Belief in God," *Religious Studies* 28, no. 3 (1992): 401.

representation of a belief is not actively and consciously involved.[64]

If a lecturer tells the students that there will be an examination tomorrow, the students will likely believe the expected examination in an *occurrent* manner, that is, actively conscious of it as something that will happen. But they may believe that tomorrow will come in a *dispositional* manner, that is, holding to the belief that a tomorrow (in which there will be examination) will surely come with no active and conscious expectation of it. This is why their expectation of the examination will be more intense in their thoughts and interest than the possibility of waking up the next day (which is tomorrow). Their belief in tomorrow (that there will be tomorrow the next day) is a disposition of their mind on the presumption of its certainty with little active consciousness. But their belief in the coming examination will be occurrent and continually active in their consciousness.

When a person *actively* and *attentively* believes or thinks of something, his belief is said to be occurrent. But if his attitude over an object of belief is only hypothetical, potential, or even presumptuous without active attention, then it is dispositional. This is the reason some epistemologists also argue that the disposition to express a belief qualifies as holding such a belief.[65] Such a disposition of the mind is not the same thing as when one actively and consciously holds to a belief.

Belief can also be full or partial. In the former, there is an attitude of all-or-nothing in the acceptance of a

---

[64] Cf. Matthew Frise, "Eliminating the Problem of Stored Beliefs," *American Philosophical Quarterly* 55, no 1 (2018): 63.
[65] Cf. The Stanford Encyclopedia of Philosophy. s.v. "Belief."

proposition or position. But in the latter, there is some gradation or degree of what one believes. Partial belief is associated with levels or degrees of belief, otherwise called credence.[66] Here, the higher the degree of a belief, the more reliable or certain the believer is, on a proposition being true.[67] The intermediate degrees (partial belief) towards the possibility of a full degree can be seen as subjective probabilities for a certainty yet to be established.[68] One may have belief of degree 0.9 that the sun will rise tomorrow. Such a belief (partial and probable) means that the believer thinks that the probability of the sun rising tomorrow is 90%. In some cases, however, higher degree of probability of belief can be seen as full belief and not partial belief. Where *partial* beliefs are basic and above a certain level, like above 0.9, a belief can be considered as full belief.[69]

Related to the degree of probability of whether a belief is partial or full is the degree of disposition. There can be partial or full belief regarding one's disposition in accepting or rejecting a position or proposition. That one has 0.7 disposition in accepting a certain proposition implies that one is 70% certain about such a proposition. The higher the degree of probability or disposition, the higher the reliability and certainty of a belief. But the lower the degree of probability or disposition, the lower the level of certainty and reliability of a proposition. Conversely, the lower the

---

[66] Cf. Erik J. Olsson, "Bayesian Epistemology," *Introduction to Formal Philosophy* (2018): 431.
[67] Cf. Stephan Hartmann "Bayesian Epistemology, " *The Routledge Companion to Epistemology* (London: Routledge, 2010), 609ff.
[68] Cf. Richard Pettigrew, "Precis of Accuracy and the Laws of Credence," *Philosophy and Phenomenological Research* 96, no. 3 (2018): 749.
[69] Cf. The Stanford Encyclopedia of Philosophy, s.v. "Formal Representation of Belief."

degree of probability or disposition, the higher the degree of doubt, uncertainty, and flexibility associated with the proposition. What this implies is that a proposition is more stable and veritable, depending on its higher degree of probability and on the higher degree of disposition of the believer. On the contrary, a proposition is more flexible and can easily be changed on the arrival of new evidence, when the degree of probability and disposition of belief is low.

Belief can also be individual or collective. The former refers to a person's belief in a proposition or position, while the latter concerns a group or community's belief. This is why you can hear people say, "I believe" or "we believe." Collective or general belief inheres in social groups as opposed to individual belief. It has to do with the joint commitment of several people as a body to accept or reject a particular belief. The nature of belief as individual or collective is related to the discussions by holists and atomists on the notion of belief. They are also related to the debate between internalism and externalism on belief.

Holists argue that the content of an individual belief depends on or is determined by collective or general belief. On the contrary, the atomists hold that individual belief is independent of collective belief. In the similar stream of logic, internalists agree with the atomists that personal or individual belief depends on what is internal to the believer and not on external things like the environment or experience and belief of others. Internalists argue that belief is shaped entirely by what goes on inside a person's mind, which is why their stance is inclined to individual belief. The externalists, however, favor holistic and collective belief theory by maintaining that external factors, including others' beliefs, play roles in shaping individual beliefs. This includes the influence of culture, which can shape our beliefs through social norms, traditions, and shared values.

Beliefs can also be classified based on the grounds of their justification. There can be belief that is vague when there is no concrete ground to support it. Uju, for instance, may believe that drinking two bottles of beer every morning makes her brilliant in class, with no scientific fact or evidence for that. If you ask her to prove the belief, she might be unable to do that. It is just what she believes in. There are many such beliefs in our daily lives and traditions where a person or a people feels something with no evidence to justify what they believe in. The most they can answer if you ask about their reason for the belief is to tell you that it is what they feel or that it is the tradition. Such cases of belief with zero evidence support are examples of vague belief.

Vague belief can be seen in individual and collective forms of belief. Vague belief is often inclined to obscurantism, whereby a person or a people could disbelieve scientific truths with clarity and evidence and rather believe unscientific truths with no reason or fact for their beliefs. It is also assisted by religiosity and traditionalism, in which people hold to some beliefs based on faith (doctrine) and tradition (native authority) with no apparent justification for their beliefs by any evidence of fact or reason. Vague belief is often unscientific and blind in logic.

Another kind of belief is one that has evidence of fact or reason to support it. In belief with well-supported evidence, some reasons, even if not proved beyond doubt, can be used to support what one believes. If I believe that the Ogui soccer team which the Bigard team played against yesterday, was a difficult team to beat because the Bigard team could not beat them, with all their hard work and good players in the football pitch, it will be a case of belief that is well-supported by fact or reason. The fact that the Bigard team did not beat them is one supporting evidence, and a reason to my belief. However, my belief, though has support of evidence, yet it is possible that my evidence is not true.

The Bigard team could also be a weak team, even with all their hard work on the pitch. And their good players may not be good enough. In that case, their inability to beat the Ogui soccer team may not be enough evidence to rate the Ogui team as a difficult team to beat. Probably, if they played against a better team than the Bigard team, they could be beaten and not rated highly.

In another example, if many of my students fail their examinations on a subject, their failure might well support a belief that the examination was difficult to pass. But it might not always be true because it could also be that the students did not study enough. In this case the belief is well supported but not beyond reasonable doubt.

There could also be belief beyond reasonable fact. This is where a belief is supported by a fact that cannot be doubted for some strong reasons. If I watched the live scene of a car crash along 87th Avenue in Westchester, Miami, I have a reason *beyond doubt* to believe it. In this case, belief with such compelling evidence beyond doubt becomes true knowledge. Facts of proof can establish beliefs beyond doubt and reasons beyond contradiction. Suppose a belief, for instance, is based on principles of identity, non-contradiction, etc. In that case, it might be so reliable that not believing it contradicts logic and reality.

When a belief is built on self-evident truth, it will be so evident that its denial results in self-contradiction. It would be self-contradictory and even absurd for me not to believe that I am sitting on a chair and typing on my laptop when, in truth and reality, it is the case. This is why beliefs beyond doubt are always true until new evidence or reason can counter them. And being true, they will constitute the fundamental nature of knowledge as true belief. But even when knowledge is seen as true belief, its truth will still rest on being justified to be relied on. However, to further comprehend the nature and arguments that have shaped the meaning of belief, some schools of thought have emerged around the discussion. Some of them include:

representationalism, functionalism, dispositionalism and interpretationalism.

3.4 Schools of Thought on Belief

3.4.1 Representationalism

Representationalism holds that beliefs are mental representations. Mental representations here stand for objects with semantic properties (propositions), which have contents that refer to something that is true or false.[70] Epistemologists who favor this school argue that beliefs are representations of ways that the world could be. This school of thought posits that beliefs are mind representations because they are not sensory in nature like perceptions or episodic memories.[71] They see beliefs as propositional attitudes which are non-sensory representations of something in the mind. Beliefs are part of the internal constitution of the mind holding the attitudes. As propositional attitudes of the mind, beliefs have content and mode.[72]

The content of a belief has to do with what it is directed to as an attitude of the mind like the propositions. It is the object of belief that constitutes its content.[73] However, the content of belief is different from that of other mental or emotional attitudes like desire, hope, hatred, love, wish, fear, intention, and doubt. For example, if Giao has the belief that "it will rain today," it means that his mental

---

[70] Cf. The Stanford Encyclopedia of Philosophy, s.v. "Mental Representation."
[71] Cf. Macmillan Encyclopedia of Philosophy, 2nd ed., s,v. "Belief."
[72] Cf. Macmillan Encyclopedia of Philosophy, 2nd ed., s,v. "Belief."
[73] Cf. Encyclopedia Britannica., s.v. "Philosophy of Mind-Propositional Attitudes."

attitude toward the proposition that "it will rain today" is affirmed to be true. This is unlike if Marile has the desire or wishes that "it will rain today." In the desire of Marile, there is no affirmation of the proposition that "it will rain today." Rather there is the involvement of the possibility of change, flexibility or wish in the mental representation of Marile. This is why some scholars hold that beliefs have mind-to-world direction on truth; thus, belief represents the world as it is (and not as one wishes it to be).

In the two examples above, there are two different attitudes toward the same proposition: "it will rain today." These attitudes (of Giao and Marile) determine the possible change or no change in their objects. If for instance, the weather turns sunny (and it did not rain), Giao who exercised a *belief* (that 'it will rain today') might revise his attitude (belief). But Marile is not likely going to revise her *desire*, (that 'it will rain today') even if the weather turns sunny (and it did not rain). This is because her *desire* is not fixed on the real condition of the world. Her *desire* that it will rain today is a wish and intentional, and as such is not fixed or based on the condition of the world or reality as it is. *Belief* can be revised upon new evidence that changes the object of belief. But *desire* may not be revised, even upon new evidence of reality. This is why people can show *desire* over what they know to be impossible. They may just wish something would happen differently, even when they see or know the indisputably obvious reality. This is unlike belief. Holding onto *belief* in an obvious false proposition or an obvious impossibility would be both contradictory and irrational.

3.4.2 Functionalism

Functionalism is a school of thought that sees beliefs in terms of their causal roles or functions in one's acceptance of a proposition or position, and not as an internal constitution of the mind (mental representation).[74] Hillary Putman subscribes to the stance of those who see beliefs as mental states or attitudes that serve a particular function.

Functionalism holds that beliefs are causes of actions. Let us make an illustration with the Bigard seminary where the ringing of bells regulates the activities of seminarians. If the bell rings by 6 pm, and its sound at that time is associated with an invitation for Angelus prayers, the belief of a seminarian on the bell's sound at 6 pm as "invitation for Angelus prayers", is functional because it is a cause or function for an action. For the functionalists, beliefs are non-sensory motivators or causal functions for human actions. This makes beliefs different from perceptions which are sensory motivators for human actions.

However, beliefs help to bridge the gap between perceptions and actions. Perceptions cause beliefs, and beliefs cause action.[75] As in the example above, the sound of the bell (perception), causes a seminarian to accept and associate the sound of the bell at 6 pm with Angelus prayers (belief), and this eventually commands him to start saying the Angelus prayers at 6 pm (action). This is why functionalists define belief as that caused by perceptions in

---

[74] Cf. The Stanford Encyclopedia of Philosophy, s.v. "Multiple Realizability."
[75] Cf. The Stanford Encyclopedia of Philosophy. s.v. "Belief."

a certain way and which also causes action or behavior in a certain way.

3.4.3 Dispositionalism

Dispositionalism argues that beliefs are identified with dispositions to behave in specific ways. Beliefs are potential causes of behaviors or dispositions for people to act in particular ways. Roderick Chisholm, who shares this stance, sees beliefs as dispositions to act as if certain things are true. Some people have associated dispositionalist concept of beliefs as a version of functionalist beliefs. For example, a belief that there is food in the refectory is associated with the disposition to affirm this when invited to the refectory at meal hours like breakfast time, lunch time or dinner time. However, it is important to note here that this thesis does not imply that only belief or a single belief can cause a behavior. Human behavior is determined by a lot of complex factors. One may be invited at lunchtime to the refectory, and while he or she believes that there is food there at that time, his or her reason (cause) for going there may not be (to eat) food but to interact with friends that he or she might meet there. This is why some people are slow to accept that beliefs can only be viewed or be defined by their functional or dispositional roles alone.[76]

3.4.4 Interpretationism

This school of thought holds that beliefs depend on what someone or people interpret a proposition or entity to be. That is to say that beliefs are relative to people's

---

[76] Cf. The Stanford Encyclopedia of Philosophy. s.v. "Belief."

interpretation.[77] Daniel Dennett and Donald Davidson in this line of thought see beliefs as interpretative schemes for making sense of someone's actions. Interpretationists argue that we ascribe belief to something in order to predict how they will behave. It means that belief can be used to predict behavior.[78] This may imply using belief to make sense of the behavior and language of another person without an earlier knowledge of the person's language. This can be done using belief to ascribe desires to the person involved.

Interpretationism is a methodology of looking at belief where we accept that entities and propositions really have the beliefs ascribed to them. It is somehow related to eliminativism and instrumentalism about beliefs. Eliminativists like Paul Churchland hold that, strictly speaking, there are no beliefs, given that there is no phenomenon in the natural world that corresponds to our folk psychological concept of belief. And if there are no beliefs, then, what we call beliefs are mere ascriptions of the mind to interpret or accept propositions or reality. Instrumentalists somewhat subscribe to this stance of eliminativists, but with an addition that belief-ascriptions are only useful, nonetheless.[79] And this usefulness can be explained in terms of interpretationism, whereby belief-ascriptions can help one predict how entities and propositions may behave.

Irrespective of whichever school of thought one might subscribe to on the notion of belief, there have been debates among epistemologists on how belief relates to acceptance of proposition or entity and knowledge as such. Scholars have argued that acceptance may imply greater

---

[77] Cf. The Stanford Encyclopedia of Philosophy. s.v. "Belief."
[78] Cf. The Stanford Encyclopedia of Philosophy. s.v. "Belief."
[79] Cf. The Stanford Encyclopedia of Philosophy. s.v. "Belief."

involvement of voluntary control of the subject unlike in belief. Acceptance is often tied to practical action in a context than belief. This means that not every acceptance implies a belief, just as not every belief implies an acceptance.

I may only accept a standard methodology prescribed by my university when writing academic papers if it is the best that can be used. Based on my acceptance, I may not question or examine the standard methodology I have accepted as a working instrument. I may take it to comply with the rule (even when I do not believe in it). In a related manner, I can feel that my car will start as soon as I turn on the ignition without accepting it. I will check my car engine's battery head and other parts to confirm my belief. The confirmation of my belief then can lead to my acceptance of the belief that my car will start when I turn on the ignition. And if I turned on my car ignition and it started, my faith and acceptance would have been justified as valid, too. What the above illustrations underline is that there are cases in which one accepts a proposition without believing it and cases in which one believes a proposition without accepting it as such. Furthermore, the debates around acceptance and belief have also led to discussions on when and how beliefs can constitute sufficient reasons for knowledge. Thus, epistemologists have raised questions as: How does belief relate to knowledge and truth? What makes a belief true or false as the case may be? Is true belief sufficient to provide knowledge? Does a true belief still need to be further justified to become an acceptable knowledge? What and what may justify true belief to become knowledge? These questions have therefore made the idea of justification in relation to knowledge a major object of study in epistemology.

Chapter Four: Knowledge and Justification

4.1 The Idea of Justification

Justification in epistemology concerns the proof one may have for holding to a proposition or believing something. It is the reason one holds for a rationally admissible belief- the excellent reason for holding on to a belief. Such good reasons may derive from the logical reasonableness (soundness) of a proposition or the perceptual experience or evidence of the senses that one has over an object of belief. However, this does not imply that reasonableness or perceptual experience provides indubitable justification for belief. A person could be justified in forming a belief based on convincing evidence or reason that was deceiving, incorrect, and illusory. Of course, the senses can deceive one by giving a false impression. Justification might also be based on reliable scientific conclusions, trusted tradition, cultivated convention, or authoritative testimony, which are trustworthy enough to make one hold a belief in them.

Further discussions on what constitutes justification have opened reflections on epistemological schools of externalism and internalism in the formation of good grounds for belief or knowledge. Externalists hold that factors outside of the psychological states of one who gains knowledge are the main conditions of justification of belief. What this means is that justification is based on the state of the external world. Thus, the external factors outside the knower are the knowledge-yielding conditions. Although many philosophers have shared this point of view, initial works on epistemic externalism are often associated with

Alvin Goldman.[80] The positions of some philosophical naturalists like W.V. O Quine as well as the formulations of Edmund Gettier in his famous Gettier's case favored this trend of justification by extrinsic factors.

Epistemic internalism, on the other hand, holds that knowledge-yielding conditions are within the psychological conditions of one who gains knowledge. Many scholars point to Rene Descartes as a typical example of the internalist form of justification. This is because his epistemology made the psychological disposition of the mind to think clearly and distinctly the principal criterion for the justification of belief. He may have acknowledged the role of the senses in the reception of the external perception, but he does not trust the reliability of sensation in the acquisition or justification of human knowledge. It is rather the intuitive power of the mind that gives indubitable knowledge through the methodic doubt of the *res cogitans*. Descartes could doubt the senses and the external world, but not his own existence as a thinking thing. The thinking self (*res cogitans*) for him is the *punctum Archimedis* (Archimedean point) through which one exercises knowledge of things.

But on whichever basis justification may be derived, that is, from external or internal factors, the fact remains that justification is an essential element for knowledge to be achieved. It is a necessary factor for knowledge, even though it may not alone be sufficient to establish knowledge. Belief and truth will also be necessary or required to establish knowledge. The necessity of these three significant factors in knowledge: belief, justification,

---

[80] Cf. Stanford Encyclopedia of Philosophy. s.v. "The Analysis of Knowledge."

and truth, is a major point of discussion and debate among epistemologists. Some have argued that the simplest definition of knowledge is that it is a justified true belief. Others have doubted this stance, starting from Russell to Gettier whose article raised the controversial question: Is knowledge justified true belief?

4.2 Is Knowledge Justified True Belief?

As noted above, the criterion for something to qualify as knowledge does not just rest on the fact that one believes it. It is also necessary that there is sufficient ground on which to base one's belief, and the belief must equally be true.[81] The ground to base one's belief is what justifies a belief to be true knowledge or not. And debates around the justification of belief as knowledge have been very loud among epistemologists. It started from its seminal assertion by Plato, to the controversies related to the same topic in contemporary times, leading to what has come to be identified as the *Gettier Problem* in epistemology.

The idea of knowledge as justified true belief is as old as the time of Plato. However, it was in the modern era of Enlightenment that it was adopted as the preferred definition of knowledge. This adoption was mainly to counter the medieval notion of knowledge as divine revelation, that is, knowledge as revealed true belief. Thus, in the spirit of Enlightenment era, the word "justified" replaced the word "revealed" in the grounding of true belief as knowledge. This is why Eboh writes that since this time till contemporary era, "the most widely accepted definition of knowledge has been that which describes it as a 'justified

---

[81] Cf. Hamlyn, *The Theory of Knowledge*, 101.

true belief"."[82] Thus, from the post-medieval era till contemporary times, knowledge has been widely accepted as Justified True Belief, otherwise symbolized as JTB.

4.3 Justified True Belief (JTB)

Knowledge as justified true belief implies that knowledge is a species of belief, though some epistemologists argue that there are certain types of knowledge that are not types of belief. People like Gilbert Ryle in this light have made distinctions between *knowing-how* to do something like driving a car and *knowing-that* some propositions are true. This corresponds to a distinction in contemporary psychology between semantic or declarative knowledge and procedural knowledge. While *knowing that* something is the case (semantic) may be a belief, it is not easy to hold that *knowing how* to drive a car (procedural) is a belief. What this means is that *knowledge-that* can mean *belief-that*, but *knowledge-of-how* cannot mean *belief-on-how*. At least, there is no readily apparent relationship between *knowledge-how* and *belief-how* in epistemology as in *knowledge-that* and *belief-that* in justifying human knowledge. If I say that I know how to drive a car, it may not necessarily be a belief. But if I say that I know that Egede is in Enugu, it necessarily constitutes a belief (of the proposition). This is why making a clear distinction between knowledge and belief is a significant part of the discussion on knowledge as JTB, which dates to Platonic epistemology.

---

[82] Eboh, *Theory of Knowledge*, 7.

In his dialogues, *Theaetetus* and *Meno*, the foundation for discussions on knowledge as JTB was laid.[83] In *Theaetetus* for instance, Socrates looked at some theories as to what knowledge is and excluded mere belief without justification from true knowledge. If one expects a special visitor on a Christmas day by mere act of the will or optimism, with no clear reasons for expecting the coming of the visitor, and then, by coincidence such a visitor comes on the Christmas day, it may not be said that one had the knowledge that such a visitor is coming, because there is no justification for that. It will at best be called best guess or coincidence. However, Plato later talked about knowledge as true belief where there is an account that explains or defines a belief in some ways. This was then called "justified true belief" (JTB) by subsequent epistemologists after him, especially in the modern and contemporary periods of philosophy.

Justified true belief means that a given proposition or belief is true, not only because one believes that but because there is a good reason for one to do that.[84] What this implies is that no one would gain knowledge or claim to know something just by believing something that happened to be true, without good justification.[85]

In JTB account of knowledge, epistemologists hold that one has knowledge of a proposition if and only if it is true, and if one is justified in believing that. Such justification of knowledge might include evidence, reason, experience, and so on. It means that knowledge can be conceptually

---

[83] Cf. Plato, "Meno," in *Classics of Western Philosophy,* ed. Steven M. Cahn (Indianapolis: Hackett Publishing, 1977), 4-27.
[84] Cf. Seth Benardete, *The Being of the Beautiful* (Chicago: The University of Chicago Press, 1984), 169.
[85] Cf. Benardete, *The Being of the Beautiful,* 175.

analyzed as Justified, as True, and as Belief. If a proposition says: "Florence knows that there is traffic at Zik's Avenue by 8am", the sentence can only be knowledge on the necessary and sufficient conditions that: S {\displaystyle S}

1. A subject (S)-Florence knows that a proposition (P)- there is traffic at Zik's avenue by 8am this morning- is true (T), if and only if,

2. P is T, and

3. S believes that P is T, and

4. S is justified in believing that P is T (given that she experienced it by 8 am this morning or heard of the traffic at Zik's Avenue by 8 am this morning through a reliable source or testimony).

It is important to note that JTB is mainly based on propositional knowledge, that is, *knowledge-that* and not mainly on *knowledge-how* or *knowledge by acquaintance*.[86] In knowledge as JTB therefore, three major conditions are seen as necessary for knowledge of something to be established: belief, truth, and justification. For knowledge to exist means that: Firstly, a person must *believe* that P (proposition) is (a fact). Secondly, that *belief* in P needs to

---

[86] Epistemologists generally agree that knowledge could be propositional (knowledge of facts), procedural (knowledge of skills) and by acquaintance (knowledge of objects or place). Thus, making an important distinction between three different senses of "knowing" something. There can be "knowing-that" something is the case, like in the truth of propositions. There can also be "knowing-how", like understanding how to perform certain actions or skills, and there can be "knowing by acquaintance", which refers to how we perceive an object or place, coming in contact with it, being familiar with it or experiencing it." Cf. Bonnie Talbert, "Knowing Other People," *Ratio* 28, no. 2 (2015): 190, and Matthew Benton, "Epistemology Personalized," *The Philosophical Quarterly* 67, no. 269 (2017): 813.

be *true*. If the *P* is false, incorrect, or mistaken, it does not matter how a person believes or feels about it, it will still not qualify as knowledge. Thirdly, a person's true belief *P* must be supported by evidence, by sound reasoning, or by any other form of rational or factual justification. If a true belief is not justified, as could happen in lucky guess, it might be correct, without being knowledge. It might be something else but not knowledge. In JTB theory of knowledge, one accepts a claim as a belief, and if that accepted claim corresponds to how things are, it becomes a true belief, and if that true belief has proper evidence, then it is justified, therefore, a justified true belief (knowledge). It basically argues that knowledge is equivalent to justified true belief. If these three conditions (justification, truth, and belief) are met over a given claim, then such a claim is taken to be knowledge.

The three conditions of JTB are individually necessary and jointly sufficient for something to be a knowledge of a proposition. What this means is that each may be necessary for there to be knowledge, but none of them alone is sufficient to account for knowledge. If for instance one believes that president Buhari was transmuted into a Sudanese called Jubril, such mere believe is insufficient to be called knowledge. For it to be knowledge, it must be established that it is true, and the truth of such a claim must be supported by evidence. Contrary to these conditions, the assertion could be anything else but not knowledge. JTB is the general form for something to be called knowledge according to many epistemologists. As necessary condition, each of them must be present for one to know something, and as sufficient condition, the three of them must be present in a proposition, for a position to be taken as knowledge.

For the above example to be knowledge, Florence has to *believe* that there is traffic at Zik's Avenue by 8am, her *believe* has to be *true* that there was traffic at Zik's Avenue by 8am, and this has to be *supported by the evidence* that she experienced it or that she was reliably told that there was traffic at Zik's Avenue by 8am. A subtraction of any of these conditions will not attest that she knows that there was traffic at Zik's Avenue by 8am. However, what constitutes one of these conditions, that is, *justification* has been a point of more discussions and further debates on JTB and has occupied the thoughts of epistemologists until the explosive thoughts of Edmund Gettier threw a big doubt on the issue of JTB. This is what has become identified in epistemology as *Gettier Problem*.

4.4 The Gettier Problem

The 1963 two-and-half page article of Edmund Gettier: "Is Knowledge Justified True Belief?" ushered in a significant debate on the arguments about knowledge as JTB. Seminal elements of similar debate, however, existed in some Platonic dialogues like *Meno* (97a-98b) and *Theaetetus*.[87] And works of Ludwig Wittgenstein, Alexius Meinong and Bertrand Russell were equally occupied with the theme in some ways. Wittgenstein's works have raised questions on JTB. Later, Russell in his 1948 book: *Human Knowledge: Its Scope and Limits* gave an example that anticipated Gettier's analogy in his example of a stopped clock. He writes in this regard:

---

[87] Cf. Plato, "Theaetetus," in *Plato: Complete Works*, eds. John M. Cooper and D. S. Hutchinson (Indianapolis: Hackett Publishing Co., Inc., 1997), 223.

Knowledge is a sub-class of true beliefs: every case is a case of true belief, but not vice versa. It is amazingly easy to give examples of true beliefs that are not knowledge. There is the man who looks at a clock which is not going, though he thinks it is, and who happens to look at it at the moment when it is right; this man acquires a true belief as to the time of day but cannot be said to have knowledge.[88]

What Russell meant in this position is that there could be a proposition which is a true belief but may fail to count as knowledge as in the case of a non-functioning clock. If Obid enters his house by afternoon hours and looks at his wall clock and sees the hand of the clock pointing at 2:00 pm. He will believe that the time is 2:00 pm. Given what he sees at the wall clock, his belief is true, and it is, in fact, 2:00pm by the conventional time of that moment (or even by a confirmation on a wristwatch). Thus, he is justified in believing that it is 2:00 pm. But what Obid might not know is that the wall clock is not going/functioning and has stopped working twelve hours ago while its hand is still pointing at the right time (2:00 pm) at that moment. Thus, he has a good reason for believing that the time was 2:00 pm by the indication of the hand of the wall clock at that time. Though he had an accidentally true, justified belief in the time at the wall clock, he did not know that it was merely coincidental, and it was by coincidence that he got the acclaimed knowledge of the time from the wall clock (though not functioning). That is, the ground for the justification or evidence of his claim was faulty or based on a non-going or incorrect wall clock.

---

[88] Bertrand Russell, *Human Knowledge: Its Scope and Limits* (London: George Allen and Unwin Ltd., 1948), 170-171.

In this case therefore, will Obid correctly claim that he knows the time to be 2:00pm according to the wall clock's indication? His knowledge of the time was true, and he believed that based on the evidence of what he sees (justification). But given that his justification was faulty or fortuitous, will his claim to know the correct time from the wall clock in question be correct? Is it possible for him to know the correct time of the day with a faulty wall clock? Is it impossible that his knowledge of the time is false given the faultiness of the wall clock?

In a related example, if a seminarian living in Bigard seminary, Enugu says that he knows that he will find a commuter bus to take him to the Old Park, Enugu, along the Zik's Avenue by 3am (a rare time to find commuter buses), then comes out and finds a commuter bus by then, by either coincidence or luck, would he be correct about the knowledge of that commuter bus being there at such unusual time? Instances of this kind challenge the JTB theory of knowledge.

However, it is important to note here that Russell did not put up the "non-going" clock example as a case of Gettier counterexample of JTB. This is because he had made his assessment of JTB before Gettier drafted his article in 1963. He presented it as an example of a true belief that yet was not knowledge because the proper justification was lacking. For him justification was missing. What he meant was that if one has a true belief based on dumb luck or coincidence, it does not qualify as knowledge. Knowledge requires that one comes by one's belief legitimately. Knowledge must be justified legitimately. This is slightly different from the stance of Gettier who argues that even when you have toiled and justified a true belief, it might still not be knowledge if your belief is true but based on lucky guess or coincidence. For Gettier, truth in knowledge has to be guaranteed by the evidence one has obtained, and which provided for the justification. All the same, the Russellian examination of JTB laid the foundation for the postulation of Edmund Gettier which is a more systematic challenge to JTB in what is well known in epistemology as the *Gettier case* or *the Gettier problem*.

Gettier problem is the name given to the popular counterexamples to the JTB theory of knowledge. It was named after the American philosopher, Edmund Gettier, who in 1963 authored a three-page article entitled: "Is Justified True Belief Knowledge?"[89] In this article, he posts examples which systematically countered or challenged the JTB definition of knowledge. This article became a landmark philosophical problem in epistemology, especially in the understanding of descriptive knowledge, otherwise called JTB.

JTB had enjoyed the status of epistemological orthodoxy until the Gettier problem arrived. As Alvin Plantinga observed, Gettier's break with the JTB tradition was as if a distinguished critic created a tradition in the very act of destroying it.[90] Gettier's case fundamentally changed the character of contemporary epistemology and has become a central issue in epistemology given that it raises a clear barrier to the process of analyzing knowledge. The counterexamples of Gettier are called *Gettier-cases* and related counterexamples after him are called *Gettier-type examples*. Sequel to his counterexamples, the adjective "Gettiered" is sometimes used to describe any case that

---

[89] Cf. Edmund L. Gettier, "Is Justified True Belief Knowledge?" *Analysis* 23, no. 6 (1963): 121.
[90] Cf. Alvin Plantinga, *Warrant: The Current Debate* (New York: Oxford University Press, 1993), 6-7.

purports to repudiate the JTB account of knowledge in epistemology.

Gettier tried to illustrate in his counterexamples that there are cases where individuals can have a justified, true belief as regards a claim but still fail to know. This is because the reasons for the belief, while justified, turn out to be false. By these examples, he tries to show that JTB theory of knowledge is inadequate because it does not account for all the necessary and sufficient conditions for knowledge. This situation may arise where there is a weak relationship between justification and truth as in cases of coincidence or mistaken identity or lucky guess. Given that justification requires having good reasons, these cases show that having a justified true belief is necessary but not reliably sufficient for knowledge. Luck or coincidence do not result in knowledge. We shall look at his first case, which is the most discussed one, and stretch the discussion to other Gettier-type examples for better comprehension.

4.5 The First Gettier Case and Gettier-Type Examples

The first case of Gettier is his postulation of the case of two men who are applying for a job: Jones and Smith. Smith has been told with assurance by the President of the company where they applied that the person who will get the job has 10 coins in his pocket (clue as reason 1). While they were waiting for the interview, Smith saw Jones count 10 coins from his pocket (observation as reason 2). Having been told by the company President that the person who will get the job has 10 coins in his pocket, and he saw Jones count 10 coins from his pocket, he believes that Jones will get the job. Thus, he is justified in inferring and believing that Jones will get the job. But in the end, it is Smith who gets the job.

Smith himself unknowingly has 10 coins in his pocket. In this case, Smith's belief that the man who will get the job has ten coins in his pocket is true (even though he did not know that he has 10 coins in his pocket). So, how did it happen that with the clue (reason 1) and his observation (reason 2), he still did not know who would get the job? And even the company President may not have also known who will get the job. He had true belief based on supported evidence or justification in the two reasons 1 and 2, yet he did not have sufficient or correct knowledge of who would get the job.

The interpretation of this illustration by Gettier is that it contains a belief which is true and justified, but which is not sufficient to be knowledge. And if that is the case, then JTB is false. This means that it is possible for a belief to be true and justified and still cannot be knowledge. That is, the combination of truth, belief, and justification does not entail knowledge automatically. A belief being true and justified may be necessary but not sufficient for it to be knowledge. Gettier has other cases of this counter argument to JTB, but we limit ourselves to this first case, while we present other Gettier-type cases by other epistemologists following in his steps.

In a 1966 scenario known, Roderick Chisholm posited the case of "The sheep in the field", where he draws an imaginary scene in which someone, Mr. X, is standing outside a field looking at something that looks like a sheep. The thing looking like a sheep is a dog disguised as one. Mr. X believes there is a sheep in the field, and, in fact, he is right because there is a sheep behind the hill in the middle of the field. Hence, Mr. X has a justified true belief that there is a sheep in the field.⁹¹ But does he know about it? Is his belief that there is a sheep in the field true, given what he sees-a dog in sheep clothing/disguise? Does he really know that there is a sheep in the field given what (dog-in-sheep-disguise) he sees?

There was also the scenario of Brian Skyrms on "The Pyromaniac." Here, there is a scene in which a man reaches out for his box of matches and, given that the clear air is dry, and the match box is dry with the usual appearance of the *match substances*, he believed that it would light when he plucks it. He then plucks the match box and it lights. However, what he does not know is that there had been some contaminations of the match box that could have made it not to light, but there had been a sudden Q-radiation which had developed from a mix of the new corrupt substance that has made the match to light. Meanwhile the man believes that it was the usual match elements that has sparked light. His belief was true and justified. But is his knowledge based on the circumstances involved? This is because the plucked match lighted, though not for the reasons of the *match substances*. It lighted because there are some unknown "Q radiation" involved.⁹² Unknowingly to him, he could have based his knowledge of lighted match on *match substances* (which is not the case).

There is also the counterexample of Alvin Goldman in his scenario of "fake barns." In this case, a man is driving in a farm village and sees what looks like barns. He thinks he is seeing barns, and, in fact, it is true that he is seeing barns. But unknown to him, the neighborhood consists of

---

⁹¹ Cf. Roderick M. Chisholm, *Theory of Knowledge* (New Jersey: Prentice-Hall Inc. 1977), 23.
⁹² Cf. Brian Skyrms, "The Explication of 'X knows that p,'" *The Journal of Philosophy* 64 no. 12 (1967): 373.

many fake barns (barn facades), which the villagers designed to look exactly like real barns when viewed from the road, and this was done to please visitors. And among the fake barns were *a few* real barns too. Thus, his belief of looking at many barns is true and justified but not correctly founded.[93] He cannot therefore claim with certainty that he was looking at *many* barns along the farmland.

In the Bigard seminary, Enugu, a seminarian, enters the chapel to pray; and from the rear of the chapel where he is, he looks at the central altar at some distance away and sees a priest of average height with light skin celebrating Mass at the central altar where the Rector, often celebrates his Masses. The Rector is of average height and light skinned. The seminarian infers and concludes that it is the Rector celebrating Mass at the central altar. Meanwhile, unknown to him, the Rector is actually celebrating in the same chapel but by the side altar which the seminarian does not see, the reason being that the Spiritual Director, had come earlier and started celebrating Mass at the central altar where the Rector had always celebrated. The Spiritual Director is equally light-skinned and of average height.

When the seminarian is done with his prayers at the rear of the chapel, while coming out, he meets the Students' Dean, at the entrance steps of the chapel. The Students' Dean asks the seminarian if he *knows* where the Rector is and what he is doing at that time. The seminarian responds that he *knows* that the Rector is in the chapel and that he is celebrating Mass in the chapel (based on whom he has seen celebrating Mass at the central altar of the chapel). Shortly after, the Rector comes out from the chapel and joins them

---

[93] Cf. Alvin I. Goldman, "Discrimination and Perceptual Knowledge," *The Journal of Philosophy* 73, no. 20 (1976): 771.

at the entrance steps, thus affirming that the response of the seminarian is true. Upon this, the Students' Dean believes that the seminarian *knew* where the Rector had been and what he was doing. The Rector coming out of the chapel has justified the belief too. And it is true that the Rector had been celebrating Mass in the chapel by the time the Students' Dean had asked the seminarian about him. Therefore, the seminarian's response shows that he *knew* where the Rector had been and what he was doing, based on justified true belief. But the problem with his *knowledge* about the Rector in this narrative is that it is Gettiered.

Is the testified knowledge of the seminarian that he knew where the Rector was and what he was doing based on correct justification? Is it not a case of mistaken identity or conflicting impressions of two people that look alike? Was it the Rector that the seminarian saw celebrating Mass in the chapel, upon which he based his answer to the Students' Dean? His knowledge of where the Rector was and what the Rector was doing might be a justified true belief, but its justification is faulty. It is based on mistaken identity and coincidence. The seminarian's knowledge about the Rector was rooted in wrong evidence/inference. The veracity of his information was coincidental and fortuitous. The seminarian cannot correctly be said to have known where the Rector was at that time (even though his claim was true) because the grounds of his claim and its justification were only fortuitous and coincidental. It is a typical case where JTB may be necessary to be taken as knowledge, but insufficient for it, because it is a Gettier-type example which counters JTB.

4.6 Explanations of Gettier's Case and Gettier-Type Examples

Gettier's cases are counterexamples that attempt to prove that some justifications which are true beliefs can be flawed and are incorrect, that is, may have become true by sheer luck and coincidence. Most Gettier-type cases are built on false beliefs, which leave them insufficiently justified. They are attempts to prove that there are cases of beliefs that are both true and justified, therefore satisfying the three conditions for knowledge in the light of the JTB account, and still do not appear to be cases of knowledge. Gettier's cases argue that JTB is false, and demand that a different theory is needed to correctly define what knowledge means.

However, Gettier, even in his typical cases, did not or was unable to satisfy this lacuna. He did not say what knowledge is if it is not JTB. He simply raised and left a dilemma against the conventional explanation of knowledge as JTB without solving it. However, he acknowledged that the three conditions: belief, truth and justification are necessary conditions for knowledge but are not sufficient as a unity for knowledge. He was equally unable to provide a sufficient condition for knowledge in his arguments. What he did was to posit that the definition of knowledge as justified true belief could be adjusted to firmer definition. This is because the premises or justification of knowledge as JTB might rest on false grounds as seen in his counterexamples.

But the question is: How does one know which premises are true or false in the definition of knowledge? This is more serious given that most of the premises can be reasonable enough to believe and be true, even though unknown to the believer, they may be faulty. How then and to what extent does one need to go on proving and accepting a belief as either true or false? Is there an indubitable criterion necessary and sufficient for a certain premise to form a true belief from which the conclusion of knowledge can be made? And in some of Gettier cases, what one observes is that the grounds or premises for the justification of a belief were weak or thin.

In the case of Smith and Jones, the argument that it is the "man with 10 coins in his pocket" was not enough or compelling evidence to believe or know that Jones will get the job. It would rather have been robust evidence, if the proposition that the man who will get the job has 10 coins in his pocket and his name is Jones. In that case, the justification would be strong and not descend to a weak ground of justification. Weak justification can be subject to dubious or false premise. If the logical derivation that made Gettier cases possible were altered, with no intentional or wrong inference, the cases would not arise. That is, where the belief is strong, and its justification is based on more reliable and solid evidence, the Gettier counterexamples would not emerge. Where the evidence is vital to be a *truth-maker*, it will be sufficient to justify true belief as knowledge without being Gettiered. Where there is thick evidence and a thick belief, the Gettier problem will not emerge, which means that JTB is still credible and reliable in some cases.

On another note, though there are differences in the details of many Gettier cases, there are also some basic elements associated with virtually all of them. The first is that each Gettier case has a fallible justification base. The support of evidence provided by most of the cases for the truth of the belief in question is not perfect, properly speaking. This is why their justifications leave open possibilities for the beliefs to be false or unreliable. The beliefs may indicate that its object is true without proving it conclusively and convincingly. Within most Gettier cases, though the beliefs may be true, their truth and justifications are often quite fortuitous, that is, built on luck. And true knowledge is not supposed to be based on luck but on rational or evidential justification. In any case, the Gettier problem since 1963 has given many epistemologists challenges and as such have spurred them into reactions and efforts at finding means to repair its impairment on the JTB. We shall examine these attempted solutions to Gettier problem.

4.7 Attempted Solutions to the Gettier Problem

Given that the two main factors that produce a Gettier case include the fallibility of justification and luck, some scholars have argued that where justification is built on a thicker ground, and where fallibility and fortuitousness are not allowed, then JTB will be stronger and Gettier possibility will be absent. Those who share this *Infallibility* stance believe that the Gettier cases can be eliminated if one refuses to allow fallibility of belief in satisfying one's JTB justification. This school of thought posits that should JTB be modified to say that no belief is knowledge if the justificatory support of the proposition is false, then the Gettier possibility will be eliminated. Where the supporting evidence has no false option, the Gettier case will not arise by any means. This position is termed a *No False Evidence Proposal* by some epistemologists.

This proposal posits that one needs to strive to establish a Cartesian certainty on what one considers the evidential or rational support for one's true belief. For those who share this standpoint, there is no justification at all where there is insufficient ground or weak ground for justification. In that case, the "justification" in JTB should not be subject to fallibility and as such need not be exposed to any Gettier weak possibility.

But the problem with this solution is that perfect certainty is not possible, even from the nature of the means of establishing knowledge. The senses and the objects of knowledge for instance are not so reliable that one can hope to obtain knowledge through them with perfect certainty. Neither we nor our objects of knowledge possess infallible justificatory criteria. But this should not imply accepting that we have only fallible justifications, as this will only lead to another drastic attitude of absolute skepticism against knowledge entirely. How it may lead to unwelcome skepticism is that it will be difficult to have a pure, no false evidence in a normal world, and if one needs to wait for such a pure justification before one accepts to know, then, one might never accept to know anything eventually.

Thus, one must maintain an epistemic balance in accepting that we know, but not that we can know with absolute certainty. In the same manner, our means and objects of knowledge can be justified but not absolutely. That is the nature of human knowledge. It is neither perfect nor purely imperfect or corrupt. The real world in which we live and which we know is a world where no belief with no single falsity exists. In our daily thinking and in our various dimensions of belief, elements of unavoidable falsity beyond our control do exist. Complete immunity of belief from impurity is nearly, if not wholly, impossible. This is why this school of thought suffers a big setback. And sometimes, the presence of a minute false belief amidst larger true beliefs may not make a justification false.

Imagine a case where five persons gave their testimony about a crime, and where four persons' testimonies are true (because they were eyewitnesses of the event) and only one who may not have been present during the crime gave the same testimony as the other four, thereby, somehow, lying (as he was not an eyewitness of the crime). Though he was lying, the overwhelming true testimony of the other four who really witnessed the crime is sufficient to sustain the testimony of the entire five on that report (proposition) that there was a crime. Even though one of them was lying because he was only affirming the testimony of the others while he was absent during the crime, it does not render the justification of the case based on the entire five testimonies false.

There is another group of epistemologists who argue that the Gettier problem can be resolved by the addition of a fourth condition to JTB. This set of scholars acknowledge the problem raised by Gettier counterexamples and affirms that JTB though is *necessary,* but they are not *sufficient* conditions for knowledge. They argue that in a case where there is JTB+...? (a fourth factor), there will be no Gettier problem. Thus, there will be an adequate set of criteria that are both necessary and sufficient for knowledge. But the next question on this attempt is on finding that adequate *fourth factor* (?) which could be added to JTB. Some have argued that a joint condition of "no-Gettier-problem" factor can be assembled to fortify justification.

Others have suggested that such a fourth factor could be found in the causal condition of belief. Where the truth of the belief has, in an appropriate manner caused the subject to believe without error, the object of his knowledge, a Gettier case will not arise. They suggest that the Gettier problem arises when there is abnormal causality of a belief. But where a necessary part of knowledge is produced in a stable and normal causal pattern that generates the belief of knowledge, there may not arise the Gettier problem. The Gettier case may come up where pattern of normality that generates the belief of knowledge is absent. JTB will not be questioned if those aspects of the world which make it true are appropriately involved in causing the belief of knowledge.

There is also the school of thought which proposes that "indefeasibility" could be added to JTB. The idea behind this "no defeat proposal" is that JTB should be modified in such a way that any defeater (fact or reason that cancels or weakens a justificatory support) of justification of belief should not be overlooked. They hold that a justified true belief will count as knowledge if, and only if, it is also the case that there is no further truth, known to the subject, which could defeat the present justification of belief. But how does one satisfy this possibility of "epistemic indefeasibility" in human fallibility? It is near impossible and unrealistic too. Given the complexity in the nature of human knowledge and environment of understanding, how thorough and strict can one be, to avoid the presence of this "defeater" element against justification?

Related to this argument are those who suggest that what Gettier used in his examples are premises with defeasible positions, and as such cannot be counted as genuine justifications (probably are some kinds of weak justification), because they have poor justificatory grounds of belief.

Another major reason a Gettier case is not knowledge is that its truth is fortuitous, that is, based on chance or luck. Thus, though luck may be powerful in deciding knowledge, it is more intuitive than rational or evidential. It cannot be a sufficient support to justify true belief. Some epistemologists have argued that if luck is eliminated in the analysis of a proposition, then, the Gettier possibility will be evaded. What this meant is that a belief is not knowledge, if it is true, only on the courtesy of some relevant luck or fluke. In this case, a belief can only be justified as true, if no luck or fluke is allowed in its justificatory situation. Its truth must be entirely predictable and inescapable and, as such, infallibly justified. Of course, this is very much like the argument on infallibilism which is utopic and unrealistic. It is not possible to eliminate the entire element of weak accidents in human acts, of which knowledge is one. What would rather be more prudent to accept is that one must avoid too much luck or flukiness to decide one's belief. Its total elimination might be unrealistic or utopian.

In all, given the various responses and solutions attempted by many epistemologists on Gettier's cases, one might also go down to a more fundamental common insight by asking: How if the ground for justification is built on lies, whereby the reason for Smith's believing that Jones will get the job is built on his boss who could have lied to him. In this case, the true belief was never justified but was rather "unjustified/flawed" on a lie that has the appearance of justification. A situation whereby the testimony of the boss of Smith is declined as convincing evidence, will make the Gettier problem inexistent. The case arose because the boss of Smith was considered reliable and trustworthy. But where he is judged to be lying or deceitful, Gettier's challenge will not arise.

These explanations notwithstanding, the theme still leaves problems on the definition of knowledge and more issues in epistemology. Is there a better formula of knowledge yet, if the JTB is questioned or rejected? What form will such a formula take? There is little consensus on whether any set of conditions succeeds in providing a set of necessary and sufficient conditions for knowledge. Many contemporary epistemologists think that such exception-free definition is not possible, and that even if justification fails to provide the condition for knowledge, no account of knowledge has been able to provide that for the time being. Therefore, the debate continues. As we ponder these challenges, we can also see how these reflections relate to truth, which is another major element in the definition of knowledge as JTB.

Chapter Five: **Knowledge and Truth**

5.1 What is Truth?

Truth is another necessary element of knowledge. It is a condition or property in which beliefs, propositions, utterances, sentences, thoughts, things, and judgments are by reality or reason. That is to say, truth can be borne by these epistemic factors: beliefs, propositions, sentences, etc. There are various etymologies for the meaning of the word, *truth*. One of them is rooted in the Greek word *Alethia*. This term is an antonym of *Lethe,* which refers to the river of forgetfulness and oblivion in Greek legend. By implication, *lethe* in classical Greek refers to that which is hidden, concealed, or veiled. *Alethia* through the prefix-**a**/alpha privative-**a** (*alpha privativum-ἀ-*) on the word *lethe* would mean that which is not hidden, not concealed, or not veiled. Therefore, *Alethia* is the state of "unconcealedness," "disclosure," "revealing," or "unclosedness" of being, in which the reality or factuality of being is evident or in which something becomes visible and clear.[94]

On its Latin root, truth is from the term *Veritas*, which means truthfulness. Heiddgger strongly subscribes to this etymology and explains that *Veritas*, unlike the Greek *Aletheia* which means "unconcealment" has more to do with Roman virtue of "correctness" or "rightness" than "unconcealment" or unveiling of reality.[95] In this sense,

---

[94] Cf. Henry George Liddell & Robert Scott, *A Greek-English Lexicon at the Perseus Project* (Oxford: Clarendon Press, 1940).
[95] Cf. Arleen B. Dallery, Charles E. Scott & Halley P. Robert, *Ethics and Danger: Essays on Heidegger and Continental Thought Issue, 17 of Selected Studies in Phenomenology and Existential Philosophy* (New York: State University of New York Press,1992), 72.

truth would mean exposing something that is hidden in its correctness or not hiding something from its correct nature.

The *New Word Encyclopedia* traces the origin of truth to the old English "(*gi*) *triewe*, which is a cognate of old Saxon "(*gi*) *triuui*".[96] It is also rooted and related to the old High German "(*ga*) *triuwu*" which refers to "faithfulness".[97] The root term of truth is equally seen in the Old Norse *trú*, which means "faith, word of honor; religious faith, belief."[98] It connotes loyalty, honesty, good faith, sincerity, verity, and certainty. Thus, truth has to do with "faithfulness, fidelity, loyalty, veracity", and that which is in "agreement with fact or reality."

Logical propositions and languages may not be the only bearers of truth. There are many carriers of truth like myths, legends, parables, symbols, narrations, gestures, jokes, things, persons etc. A myth or parable for instance can be a carrier of truth, even though its narrative representations may not be true-by means of corresponding to factual history or rational reality. In the ancient and biblical epochs, myth, legends, parables, and other forms of anthropomorphic descriptions have been used to carry and communicate truth.

A thing or person can also be a truth-bearer. This is why one can say that a thing or a person is true (true to itself or himself/herself), like when something is genuine, or one is authentic or honest. In this case, truth would mean adherence to real nature, cause, principle, and promise. A

---

[96] *The New Word Encyclopaedia*, s.v. "truth".
[97] Ignatius Itohowo, Iniobong Umotong, Otto Dennis, "Heidegger's Notion of Truth as *Alethia*: A Critical Exposition," in *International Journal of Humanities and Innovation (IJHI)* Vol. 5 No. 2, (2022): 74.
[98] *A Concise Dictionary of Old Icelandic*, s.v. "Truth".

true wine would mean wine whose contents adhere to pure quality or nature of wine. A true believer would mean one who adheres to the correct teaching of his faith doctrines or belief system. Thus, truth implies firmness in allegiance, constancy in faith, loyalty, faithfulness, honesty, virtuousness, accuracy, correctness, sincerity, genuineness, etc.

5.2 Truth in Epistemology

Epistemologically, truth is the correspondence or coherence of thought or language to a mind-independent world or reality. Eboh defines it thus:

> Truth is the faithful adherence of our judgements and ideas to the facts of experience or to the world as it is: but since we cannot always compare our judgments with actual situations, we test them by consistency with other judgements that we believe are valid and true, or we test them by usefulness and practical consequences.[99]

What this means is that truth involves the agreement of our thoughts and judgements with obvious and objective reality, which equally is consistent with the measure of other things that are true. It is the correctness and certainty of things and propositions affirmed or affirmable in our empirical facts and rational judgements. Its certainty is part of why Plato associated it with the eternal and immutable Forms, as different from opinions which are neither conclusive nor certain in their nature. Plato, in his allegory of the divided line argued that truth is an eternal and unchangeable correct or real nature of things which exist in

---

[99] Eboh, *Theory of Knowledge*, 49.

the world of Forms, and which can be apprehended through the process of recollection or remembrance (*anamnesis*).

Aristotle, unlike Plato, would rather define truth as the intellectual adequation or correspondence of thoughts to reality (*adaequatio intellectus ad rem*). Truth in Aristotle, therefore, is a correspondence of thought or knowledge with an object or thing, where thought encompasses representation, thinking, or statement or proposition. This means that "truth is the conformity of the mind with reality, when what is in the mind conforms with what is in reality."[100] As further explained by Eboh, "truth exists as far as thought (intellect i.e., judgement) conforms objectively to what is. In short, truth is considered as 'fidelity to objective reality,' that is, the agreement between the statement of fact and actual fact or situation which the judgement claims to describe."[101] This Aristotelian notion of truth laid the foundation for the correspondence theory of truth.

Following the Platonic tradition, St. Augustine argued that truth is not in obvious reality, but it is rather an eternal and divine idea of a thing which exists in the mind of God. Our minds can only comprehend it through the power of divine illumination. Thus, Omoregbe, explaining the position of St. Anselm who followed this Augustinian notion of truth writes:

> St. Anselm who was an Augustinian defined truth as the 'the rightness of something as perceived by the mind, that is, truth lies in the mind of correctly perceiving the divine ideas reflected in things. For all things are reflections of the eternal ideas of God, the ideas in the divine mind

---

[100] Omoregbe, *Epistemology*, 40.
[101] Eboh, *Theory of Knowledge*, 41.

according to which he created things. Before God created things, he had in mind the ideas of what he was going to create, and he eventually created all things according to these ideas in mind. Thus, creatures are reflections of these ideas of God. Therefore, when the mind correctly perceives these ideas of God as reflected in things, it attains truth'.[102]

What this means is that when we perceive the divine ideas in things, we are in grasp with their truth. And the more we perceive them, the more we know their truth.

Following the Aristotelian tradition, Thomas Aquinas defines truth as "*adaequatio intellectus et re*," that is, agreement of what is in the mind with obvious reality. This is why he argues that for there to be knowledge, there must be similarity of the thing known in the knower, given that "truth is the equation of thought and thing."[103] He maintains that the first comparison of being with the intellect lies in the fact that being corresponds to the intellect. This correspondence is known as '*adaequatio*' or "conformity" of the thing and the intellect, which formally realizes the truth of the thing known. As he affirms in *De Veritate*, the truth is a conformity of thing and intellect.[104] Truth or falsity for Aquinas resides in the judgement of the intellect on reality. It is the conformity of intellect and the thing, whereby to know this conformity is to know the truth. This is such that judgement is something properly belonging to the intellect, and it is not found in the thing. But when that which exists outside the intellect corresponds to it, then judgement is said to be true.[105] When intellect makes correct

---

[102] Omoregbe, *Epistemology*, 39.
[103] Aquinas, *Summa Theologica*, q.16, 2.
[104] Cf. Thomas Aquinas, *Quaestiones Disputatae de Veritate* q.1, a.1-3.
[105] Cf. Aquinas, *Summa Theologica*, q.16°, 2.

judgement that agrees with the facts or reason of a thing or statement, truth is attained according to Aquinas. Truth pertains to the intellect and not the senses. It is a product of intelligibility primarily, and not sensitivity as such.

Years later, Heidegger criticized this idea of truth as conformity of intellect to reality. He claims that the reduction of truth to sheer relationship between the knowing-subject and known-object only exhausts the concept and its value to empirical phenomenon or state of affairs. Such an idea of truth is only understandable in the natural and social sciences. The deeper or philosophical meaning of truth, according to him, should be traced back to the ancient Greek meaning, which is *unconcealment* or *disclosedness* of being, *aletheia* or Latin *Veritas* which has to do with correctness of a thing. He did not subscribe either to the reduction of truth to rational certainty or empirical justification as seen in the modern age philosophy depicted in Rene Descartes and John Locke.

Omoregbe writes that, "For Descartes, truth is the 'clear and distinct perception' of innate ideas."[106] This means that truth is the indubitable idea of things, which comes from our introspection. It is not a product of external perception through sensation but rather of intuitive perception. He argues further by positing *the thinking self*, "I think, therefore, I am" (*cogito ergo sum*) as the first indubitable truth, from which other forms of truth are derived. Every other truth logically derives from the rational intuition of the self, which is the authentic subject of truth. And for him, the truth of the *thinking self* is indubitable and, as such, certain that it cannot change, thus, making certainty an essential ground for truth. Certainty in this case will

---

[106] Omoregbe, *Epistemology,* 39.

mean one's belief in which there is no rational ground for doubt. It is such that anyone holding a belief could not be mistaken in doing that. When there is epistemic certainty, there is infallible justification of a proposition or position (unless a new insight alters that).

Empiricists like Hume and Locke explained truth as the agreement of ideas which are products of perceptive impressions with object of understanding. When we perceive things, they leave impressions on us, which the Empiricists call concepts or ideas. These ideas are the means through which we get a knowledge of reality, and they are not exactly of the same nature as the realities themselves. This is why the Lockean conceptualism on the universals as objects of intellective understanding is a typical case of indirect realism. In indirect realism, sense impressions or concepts serve as perceptual intermediary that mediate between the perceiver and the object of perception.[107] When these sense impressions or ideas agree with the nature of the objective reality, then truth is achieved. On the contrary, when there is a disagreement between the ideas and the nature of objective reality, then there is falsity. As Omoregbe captures this in his explanation:

> The objects of knowledge are not things themselves but our ideas of them, which derive from the impressions they make on us when we perceive them. Consequently, truth has to do with these ideas, that is, the agreement and the disagreement between them.[108]

In the contemporary time, Soren Kierkegaard posits that truth is "an agreement between thought and being,

---

[107] Cf. Ani, *Topics in Epistemology*, 219.
[108] Omoregbe, *Epistemology*, 39.

where being is synonymous with reality."[109] Truth in this sense would be, either where thought conforms to being (empirical definition) or being conforms to thought (idealistic definition). He made a distinction between objective and subjective truth. However, though he accepted the correspondence notion of truth, he placed emphasis on the subject as the ground of truth, whereby truth becomes a self-identity with thought and reality in relation to the subject. Truth is essentially about how actual reality relates to the subject or the individual. As an existentialist, truth is shaped by the conditions of human subjectivity.

For Kierkegaard therefore, truth is subjective. As Jery H. Gill cited him: "What good is purely objective truth if it is not appropriated into the life of the knower?"[110] According to him, it is the relationship of the knower and the premise that puts the individual in the truth and generates a higher, subjective truth for that individual alone. In Kierkegaard, the truth is shaped by the inwardness of the subject and not by the content of the object of comprehension. There may be objective truth that resides in the object of knowing but it remains uncertain and unknown until it is made known by the consciousness and experience of the subjective, ultimately, making it a product of "subjective made" truth. Gill explains in this light that subjective truth is "an objective uncertainty held fast in an appropriation-process of the most passionate inwardness ... the highest truth attainable for an existing individual."[111]

---

[109] Soren Kierkegaard, *Concluding Unscientific Postscript: A Critical Guide*, ed. Rick Anthony Furtak (New York: Cambridge University Press, 2010), 192.
[110] Jerry H. Gill, *Essays on Kierkegaard* (Minneapolis: Burgess Publishing Company, 1969), 91.
[111] Gill, *Essays on Kierkegaard*, 96.

Gill further explains that for Kierkegaard, the attainment of subjective truth requires total act and commitment of the knower.[112] To show this commitment, one must cross through the three major stages of his existentialism, which include the aesthetic, the ethical and the religious. The aesthetic, as explained by Peter Cave is "dominated by our desires and dispositions, certainly not by any sense of duty. It is the stage where we seek interest and excitement, eager to overcome boredom."[113] It is marked by a series of idle moments, with little consistency and no sense of duty. The ethical stage puts emphasis on the universal and duty, where social roles and conventions determine ethics like commitment to work, friendship and marriage.[114]

Then, the religious stage is where one rises to a higher level and encounters one's subjectivity. It is the stage characterized by touch of the private and the personal. In this stage, one may abandon the excitements of the aesthetics and the universal duty of the ethical to make an act of faith to a higher goal like Abraham did in his obedience to God (against the ethical demand of not killing his son).[115] Cave describes it thus:

> From the sphere of the ethical, Abraham is an horrendous character in even contemplating killing his own flesh-and-blood and violating the moral duty never to murder the innocent. Abraham is, using Kierkegaard's terms, engaged in a 'teleological suspension of the ethical with his

---

[112] Cf. Gill, *Essays on Kierkegaard*, 92.
[113] Peter Cave, *How to Think Like a Philosopher* (Dublin: Bloomsbury Publishing Plc, 2023),142.
[114] Cf. Cave, *How to Think Like a Philosopher,* 142.
[115] Cf, Patricia F. Sanborn, *Existentialism* (New York: Pegasus, 1968), 120.

preparedness to obey God, despite violating some basic moral principles.[116]

Certainly, his action may sound mad, absurd, and paradoxical, but it shows how this "Knight of faith" as he calls him, relates his finite truth of temporality to God's infinite truth of eternity. The religious stage of truth is irrational and absurd, but it is the stage that provides the basis for real subjective truth or faith.[117] Senses and reason may take one some far, but subjective truth is achieved when one enters the level of the irrational and takes a leap of faith by accepting the absurdity of the higher truth without proof or ethics. Such is a level of higher truth that we can live and die for. No wonder he avows that faith is like a leap into abyss. Kierkegaard, therefore, wants to show that subjective truth commands objective reliability, passionate inwardness, and faith, which is above sensation and rationality.

In his reflections on truth, Martin Heidegger in his *Being and Time* argues that truth is grounded in the being of the human person which he technically calls the *Dasein*. According to his analysis of the ontology of truth, *Dasein* is the only being that discloses Being as such. This is because *Dasein* is the only being which questions and understands the being or essence of entities it encounters as a being-in-the-world. Through his rationality and interrogation, the *Dasein* can take the beings of other entities out of their concealment. It is one way the *Dasein* establishes his mastery over other entities, that is, being able to demonstrate and unveil their truth. Heidegger's idea of truth is more ontological than ontical as seen in his reflections on

---

[116] Cave, *How to Think Like a Philosopher*, 143.
[117] Cf. Gill, *Essays on Kierkegaard*, 92.

truth as propositional correctness. It is also expressed in the existentiality of the *Dasein* as a being in the world. This is why the truth of *Dasein* according to Heidegger is tied to his temporality and historicity. It is in his time and history that truth is revealed to him, and he remains the proper ground of that revelation.

He further posits that though the *Dasein* is the ontological ground of truth, he is also the reason for untruth of being. Given that *Dasein's* role in the unconcealment of truth takes place in his state of fallenness as a being in the world, the interplay of the factors of fallenness do hamper the process of correct revelation or disclosure of being to him. State of fallenness or thrownness of the *Dasein* is the condition of the *Dasein* as a being in the world who is limited by existential or social factors like conventions, laws, customs, habit, etc. These factors also make the disclosure of entities by *Dasein* to be "in untruth." The fact of being enmeshed in relationship with other entities traps the *Dasein* in possible uncertainties and falsity, which constitute being "in untruth." The conditions of fallenness subject the being of the *Dasein* to constant conflict between revealing and concealing of truth or correctness and falsity of being. When humankind lives in authenticity, he or she becomes a being where truth is disclosed, but if he or she lives in the inauthenticity of fallenness, he or she becomes a being where falsehood is revealed. Thus, Itowoho *et al* writes that: "*Dasein* is 'in truth' when he lives in his authentic mode; and 'in untruth' when he lives in inauthentic mode. To live in authentic mode requires man to be aware and live his true self and not hide in the 'anonymous they', the *Dasman*."[118]

---

[118] Itohowo et al, "Heidegger's Notion of Truth as *Alethia*," 76.

It is by being-in-the-world that the *Dasein* reveals the world, and through that revelation, he makes the discoverability of other beings conceivable and possible. Being or other entities would not be shown/discovered or be spoken about in proposition without the possibility of the *Dasein*. Thus, the *Dasein* as they explain is "the ontic condition of the possibility of the discovery of beings."[119] As captured by Etuk, A:

> *Dasein* (man) is the locus where truth becomes evident, since only *Dasein* can raise the question about his being or about Being itself. That is, man is the only being who becomes aware not only of his own being but being itself. Man is the only being who is capable of self-interrogation. The very fact of asking the question of being is *Dasein's* mode of being.[120]

The implication of this position is that the ontological truth of the *Dasein* is the foundation of the ontic truth of entities other than the *Dasein*. Ontic facts and propositions related to them are derived from the ontological discovery of the *Dasein*. It is humankind who discovers and declares the truth of other things in creation. Truth for Heidegger is, therefore, anthropocentric, that is, centred on, and serving man.

For Bernard Lonergan, truth is associated with insight and reasonable affirmation of reality.[121] Truth is a relation of knowing to being, in a manner that there is

---

[119] Itohowo et al, "Heidegger's Notion of Truth as *Alethia*," 76.
[120] A. Etuk, "*The Truth about Truth: Discourse on the Problem of Truth in Epistemology*," in Itohowo *et al*, "Heidegger's Notion of Truth as *Alethia*." 77.
[121] Cf. Bernard Lonergan, *Insight: A Study of Human Understanding*, ed. F.E. Crowe and R. Doran, CWL, III (Toronto: University of Toronto Press, 1992), 575.

absence of difference between knowing and what is known. It is the reasonable affirmation of an object of reality by an authentic subject of knowing. Truth for him has to do with the authenticity of the subject of understanding, who maintains the "basic horizon" in the process or intentionality for knowing.[122] This authenticity of the subject of truth implies being attentive, being intelligent, being rational and being responsible, if one has to achieve what is true (otherwise called insight or objectivity).[123] On the contrary, where one pursues knowledge with an inattentive, unintelligent, irrational, and irresponsible attitude, one is likely to end in falsity or what he calls oversight.[124] Lonergan equally argues that truth is related to what we do because knowing the truth and not following or living it out defeats the process and content too. This is why he talked about volitional appropriation of truth in which we can live up to the light of truth by a sensitive appropriation of truth, thus, adapting our sensibility to the requirements of our knowledge and responsible decisions.[125]

In Igbo epistemology, an aspect of African epistemology, truth is called "*eziokwu*." It is a compound word made up of *ezi* (rightness/rectitude) and *okwu* (word or speech)[126] Theophilus Okere analyzed the etymology of the term when he drew an analogy of it with *the uzi* tree and *ezi* (open space), which is one of the components of the compound word, *eziokwu* (truth). According to Okere, the

---

[122] Cf. Ani, *Critical History*, 157.
[123] Cf. Bernard Lonergan, *Method in Theology* (Toronto: Toronto University Press, 1972), 104.
[124] Cf. Ani, *Critical History*, 51.
[125] Cf. Lonergan, *Insight*, 577.
[126] Cf. Theophilus Okere, *Religion in a World of Change: African Ancestral Religion, Islam, and Christianity* (Aachen: Whelan, 2003), 333.

uzi tree is a popular tree in Igbo land and grows in a straight and unbending way that one would stand at its base to see its straightness to its apex, without interruption and crookedness. It often stands taller than all other trees and can live for hundreds of years. Thus, the *uzi* tree provides an analogy of straightness, smoothness, clarity, and perennity with which truth is associated and epistemically identified. Okere calls *uzi* "the tree of truth."[127]

Uzi and *ezi* share the root morphene: "zi" which stands for correctness, rightness, and rectitude as one could see in other Igbo words like ihe **zi**rie**zi** (that standing straight or right), e**zi**-uche (right-thought), e**zi**-agwa (proper behavior/rectitude), e**zi**-uzo (right way), *ezi-ndu* (good life), *ezigbo mmadu*(good person), i**zi**-ako (proper teaching), and nku-**zi** (right/correct shaping/teaching). The Igbo word for teaching is *nkuzi*, which means to shape correctly. Thus, *ezi-okwu* (right word) is the literal translation of truth, where a spoken word is right, correct, straight, unveiled, and without ambiguity. Somehow, this gives truth, not only epistemic value but ethical and existential one. It is why the Igbo people say *eziokwu bu ndu* (truth is life). Furthermore, *eziokwu*(truth) is one of the essential criteria for admission into sacred clubs in Igbo society like that of *ndi ozo*,[128] where the members are expected to be advocates and custodians of truth and justice.[129]

Another etymological account of *eziokwu* (truth) is from *ezi*, which translates as "an open space." When *ezi* is

---

[127] Okere, *Religion in a Word of Change*, 334.

[128] *Ndi Ozo* or members of Ozo society are Igbo native honorary society reputed custodians of truth and justice in the society.

[129] Cf. G.U Dine, *Traditional Leadership as Service Among the Igbo of Nigeria* (Roma: Laterenese University Press, 1983), 126.

linked to *okwu* (word or speech), the compound term *eziokwu* will literally and linguistically mean "open word or speech." In other words, it means "word said in the open" in clear terms without guile and ambiguity.[130] Such a word said in clarity unveils reality as it is. This is similar to the Heideggerian *Alethia* in, in which truth essentially represents the revelation of being. Thus, truth is constituted in words spoken in the open, in clear terms, and is acceptable because it is unambiguous. Truth from this Igbo philology is that which has the quality of openness and clarity, as can be perceived by the senses, apprehended by the intellect, and appropriated by the will. This way, truth (*eziokwu*) is linked to thoughtfulness and conscientious comprehension, otherwise termed *akonuche* in Igbo epistemology.

The idea of *eziokwu* (truth) is identified with the satisfaction of proper perception and thoughtfulness. It relates to the correspondence theory of truth, based on an open acknowledgment and representation of reality through the human experiences of perception and conception. As Amechi Udefi explains:

The Igbo attaches different epistemic certainty to experiences or propositions. In other words, what someone experiences or sees with his eyes firsthand, coupled with the mind or cognitive apprehension of it, is taken as a reliable way of knowing and is regarded as genuine (*ezi-okwu*).[131]

---

[130] Cf. N. Otakpor, *Ezi Okwu Bu Ndu: Truth is Life* (Michigan: Hope Publications, 2008), 159.

[131] Amaechi Udefi (2014). "The Rationale for an African Epistemology: A Critical Examination of the Igbo Views on Knowledge, Belief, and Justification," in *Canadian Social Science*, 10 (3), 108-117. http://www.cscanada.net/index.php/css/article/view/4445 DOI: http://dx.doi.org/10.3968/4445 1:115ff.

5.3 Practical Values of Truth

The various discussions on truth above are mainly theoretical and speculative. The fact remains that truth is essential as a human value. At an ontological level, truth helps in speculative understanding of reality in their principles. On a personal level, truth can help one in self-discovery, self-knowledge, and self-appropriation. As seen above, the moral practice of truth is very much embedded and implied in the Igbo concept of truth, *eziokwu* (righteous word and action). At a social level, truth is especially important for the sustainability of social contracts. That people believe what they are told is because they accept the truth of what they have been told.

That parents, teachers and formators can impact their authority and learning on their children and students is because they believe in the truth of what they have been told or taught. The technical and moral authority which the teachers and parents use in effecting the education of their young ones are possible because of truth. In religious beliefs, truth is particularly important for people to believe the doctrines of their various faith positions. Truth is the ground of all beliefs. In fact, truth is needed for people to thrive in various social structures of the world. It is so important in society that its absence can rattle intersubjective existence in every order. It can result in a lot of legal and social penalties and anarchy. Lack of truth can disrupt society and even cost lives. Believing what is not true for instance can spoil plans and retard scientific progress. The pursuit and progress of science, philosophy, history, economics, law, religion, etc. are only possible because of their true contents. Without truth, the credit/monetary system and general economic activities in society will not be possible. Thus, truth is an invaluable currency of ontological, existential, intersubjective, social, and spiritual weight.

However, the exercise of truth is delicate, so it has to be done with utmost prudence. But this does not imply a compromise of truth. Thus, it requires courage to speak or live out the truth, even when it might have serious consequences. Of course, people who stood for the truth had often paid grave prizes for that. Socrates and Jesus Christ are typical examples of people who have been killed insisting on the truth of what they know. Even in our world today, speaking out openly and courageously, otherwise called parrhesia, can be risky. Exercising parrhesia, whereby one honestly and bluntly speaks out the truth in the face of personal danger, out of a deep conviction, and without persuasion, falsehood, silence, flattery, diplomacy, etc., can expose one to the risk of insecurity, criticism, persecution, and even death.

5.4 Criteria of Truth

Apart from the nature and values of truth, it is also important to state that there are certain standards or rules which something or propositional knowledge needs to possess to be seen or classified as true or truth carrier.[132] These rules are the tests of truth which are used to measure the accuracy or reliability of claims and statements of truth. They are the common tools of verification or acceptance of truth. These rules are also the conditions that inform and determine what people accept as true knowledge. Of course, some of them are strong conditions that can produce reliable truth, while some are weak conditions for truth production. But there is none without some strengths or some

---

[132] These criteria of truth must not be confused with the conditions of justification of knowledge as discussed earlier.

weaknesses. These criteria include authority, consensus, coherence, consistency, correspondence, custom, utility, intuition, instinct, emotion, time, tradition, and revelation. These criteria also help in the formulation of the theories of truth like coherence, correspondence, pragmatic, consensus etc. theories of truth as we shall see later.

Authority as a criterion of truth means that the expertise or wealth of experience of certain people provide knowledge that form proof and ground for people to certify something to be true. This may not be infallible as there

Coherence is another test of truth could be conflict between authorities or new evidence challenging or invalidating the stance of an authority on an issue. [133] because it makes a particular position or proposition cohesive and consistent with the logic and order of other truth categories. It integrates a proposition or position to the logical order of others, and that is why arguing against it becomes inherently illogical and lends credence to endorsing and invalidating incoherence. It is the basis for the coherence theory of truth. Related to this factor are consistency, consensus, and correspondence. A statement is considered true for instance because it has no contradiction. It is very much assisted by the law of noncontradiction in its value of truth-making as often applied in formal logic and mathematical propositions. [134] Coherence combined with consistency might also provide the ground for consensus as a truth test.

Consensus (*consensus gentium*) is when there is a general and universal consent of all or many over a belief.

---

[133] Cf. William Sahakian & Mabel Lewis Sahakian *Ideas of the Great Philosophers* (New York: Barnes and Noble,1865). 8-9.
[134] Cf. Sahakian and Sahakian, *Ideas,* 10.

It is sometimes referred to as majority-rule test of truth, which often is used in social science like in a democracy. It is used to determine group decisions on truth over social or ethical issues. If the truth held by consensus is based on justified or inherent truth of what is believed as in ethical, mathematical, or logical rules, the value of its truth will be reliable and sustainable. But if it is based on sheer agreement of a unanimous crowd, then, it can become uncertain, unreliable, and unsustainable.[135] Correspondence in which a claim of truth corresponds to an object or fact that people can see, and experience is a strong criterion of truth which also gives the foundation for the correspondence theory of truth as championed by Aristotle and Aquinas.

Some theorists have also acknowledged other human elements as criteria of truth. People may assume that what is customary will prevent error in ethical or social decisions. This is why people can accept certain modes of behavior based on custom, and not on evidence or reason. Related to custom in this regard are time and tradition. People often appeal to the test of time as the reason for what they hold to be true. They may argue that over time, erroneous beliefs, and logical flaws could be revealed, and if a belief has stood the test of time, mere passage of time cannot affect its validity. Many people believe that the religious belief they follow is true because it has stood the test of time, and they may find it difficult to change to new ones, which they think might be untrue.[136] Time and custom often produce tradition in standard of truth. Those who propose this criterion hold that ideas that have gained the loyalty of many generations possess a measure of

---

[135] Cf. Sahakian and Sahakian, *Ideas,* 7.
[136] Cf. Sahakian and Sahakian, *Ideas,* 4-5.

credibility, and as such must be true. But this stance, just like in custom and time, is flawed because an error can be sustained in custom, time, and tradition for centuries.[137]

Emotions, instincts, and intuitions, insufficient as they might be, also form part of the criteria of truth. Some social scientists agree that there are times when people drop reason and even evidence and allow their emotions to determine what they believe to be true. Even though this may not be acceptable to reasonable and serious-minded people, it is a reality experienced in human society. The same goes for instinct which in most cases, people allow to determine what they accept to be true. Though it is often personal, variant, indistinct and subtle to be grasped, yet it serves and often motivates people to their truth.[138] Instinct is like intuition, in which one assumes truth in an unknown or possibly unexamined criteria.

Intuition as ground of truth is anchored on sensation, rashness, rushed and unthoughtful feeling and belief. It can sometimes occur as a sudden sensation without deep consideration and may later turn out to be true. Intuition is both a test and source of truth. And it is closely related to revelation. The difference between the two is that while intuition is most times believed to arise from human unthoughtful sensation, revelation is assumed to have its source in a divine entity like God, Angels, demons, deities, spirits etc. This is why it is the basis and test of many religious truths. However, both intuition and revelation are criticized on the ground that firsthand experiences of truth are inadequate criteria for proof of knowledge to others.[139]

---

[137] Cf. Sahakian and Sahakian, *Ideas*, 4.
[138] Cf. Sahakian and Sahakian, *Ideas*, 5-6.
[139] Cf. Sahakian and Sahakian, *Ideas*, 6-7.

Direct empirical sensation without discreet rational examination, usefulness, practicality, rationality etc. are among other means of testing that something or claim is true. And from these criteria, some theories of truth have been generated by philosophers and scholars of different areas of study. There are classical or principal theories of truth according to epistemologists that have flourished in the history of philosophy for centuries. They include the correspondence theory of truth, the coherence theory of truth and the pragmatic theory of truth. There have also been other (ancillary) theories of truth outside these three, which have been derived from them or from other epistemic attempts to analyze and understand truth.

Chapter Six: **Theories of Truth**

6.1 Principal Theories of Truth

Conventionally, there are three main theories of truth in epistemology as mentioned above (the correspondence theory, the coherence theory, and the pragmatic theory). There are other ancillary ones that are inspired by them as well as those that have unique or special approaches to truth. These other ones include the semantic theory of truth, the deflationist theory of truth, the minimalist theory of truth, the dialectical theory of truth, the redundancy theory of truth and the relativist theory of truth. We shall look at them specifically starting from the three main theories: correspondence, coherence, and pragmatic.

6.2 The Correspondence Theory of Truth

The correspondence theory of truth says that a proposition is true provided there exists a fact corresponding to it. In other words:

(1) A proposition p is true,

(2) if and only if p corresponds to F,

(3) F is a Fact.

The theory argues that truth is a certain relationship between a proposition and its corresponding fact. It is sometimes called the evidence or realist theory of truth. It holds that truth is the correspondence or "conformity of the intellect (judgment) to the object known (*adaequatio intellectus ad rem*)."[140] This theory was mainly influenced by the Aristotelian-Thomistic definition. But even Aristotle's position on this theory was inspired by Plato's *Sophist* and *Theaetetus* where it first featured. In the *Theaetetus*, Socrates had tried to differentiate true belief from erroneous belief, by arguing that whereas a true belief is directed at what is, a false belief is directed at what is not. But if a belief is directed at what is not, will it still be said to be directed at anything or nothing? And if it is directed at nothing, is nothing the same thing with "false thing?" To be directed at "what is not" is not the same thing as being directed at what is not true or what is false. However, his discussion in this case laid the seminal platform for correspondence theory of truth which holds that truth occurs when a belief is directed at something that is real. On the contrary, falsity is when a belief is directed at nothing (by implication, at what is not real).

Aristotle in his *Metaphysics* while defining truth writes: "To say that that which is, is not, and that which is not, is, is a falsehood; therefore, to say that that which is, is, and that which is not, is not, is true."[141] This means that true beliefs or judgements must agree or correspond to what really is, and not to the contrary. True judgements must agree with reality or the real situation in the real world. He posits that it is by facts of the case, by their being or not being so, that a statement is called true or false. He emphasized this while arguing against the idea that a statement may be at one time true and at another time false, like where "Mr. Aju is sitting down" will be true, if he is sitting down, but will be false if he stands up.

---

[140] Eboh, *Theory of Knowledge*, 41.
[141] Aristotle, *Metaphysics*, bk. 4, sec. 1011b.

Aristotle thinks that this is unfair because what is in question here is not an alteration of the statement itself but rather alteration in the facts outside it by which its truth or falsehood is measured. On another note, if I say (a) "this my white car *was* black" is true, but (b) "this my white car *is* black" is not true, the truth of these propositions is not based on the predications as such but on the time variance of the propositions. The case here is that (a) predication is true because it corresponds with the true color of my car in the past, while the (b) predication is not true because it does not agree with the color of my car which is white (not black) in the present. It was only black in the past, and not in the present. So, the correspondence of a proposition with reality has much to do with the time of prediction and reality too.

The facts and time-reference of predication do shape the truth or falsity of statements, where the proposition may not be the criteria for the veracity of a statement. Truth for this theory is mainly measured by how ideas in the mind correspond to obvious reality. Truth or falsity of a statement or judgement is determined by how it relates to the real world and how it accurately describes or corresponds with reality in the world.[142] This is also why the theory is deeply rooted in empiricism and *a posterior* judgment of propositions.

Beyond the Platonic-Aristotelian position on this, the Stoics of Ancient Greek philosophy have some teachings that also laid epistemic foundation for the correspondence theory. They held that truth is essentially the property of statement or axiomata, in the sense of what the sentence states or means. And according to them, these

---

[142] Cf. Humphrey Uchenna Ani, *Introduction to Philosophy of History* (Enugu: Snaap Press Ltd, 2021),160.

axiomata exist independent of being expressed by sentences. In this case, the meanings of sentences as either true or false exist outside the sentences themselves. The *axiomata* expressed by "It is day" is true if it is day, and false if it is not.

In the Medieval age, Thomas Aquinas used the word *correspondentia* in many ways to express his definition of truth. While citing a definition of truth he attributed to a Ninth Century Jewish Neoplatonist, Isaac Israel, he writes that "truth is the adequation of things and intellect" (*veritas est adaequatio rei et intellectus*).[143] This is in accord with the position of most Scholastics that "the thing is as signified" in reality (*ita est sicut significat*).

There are elements of correspondence theory in works of some early modern philosophers like Descartes, Spinoza, Locke, Leibniz, Hume and Kant,[144] and later modern philosophers like Marx and Joseph Schelling.[145] In contemporary times, one sees elements of this theory too in the writings of Husserl, Popper, Moore, Russell, and Wittgenstein.[146] G.E Moore for instance posits that what makes a sentence or belief true is the truth of a fact it refers to. Moore finds it more convenient to speak of beliefs as referring to facts as the criteria of veracity. Truth and falsity are properties of propositions, and propositions for him are not just indicative sentences but what a sentence means (the axiomata in the sense of the Stoics). And these propositions

---

[143] Cf. *Encyclopaedia of Philosophy*, s.v. "Correspondence Theory of Truth."
[144] Cf. *The Stanford Encyclopaedia of Philosophy,* s.v. "Correspondence Theory of Truth."
[145] Cf. Joel Harter, "Coleridge's Philosophy of Faith: Symbol, Allegory and Hermeneutics," *Religion in Philosophy and Theology* 55, no. x (2011): 242.
[146] Cf. J.L, Austin, "Truth," *Philosophical Papers*, 3rd ed. (1979): 117.

are often apprehended by us even before finding words to express them through sentences.

When one says that a belief is true or false, the word belief is not used to represent the *act of believing* but the *fact believed* in the primary sense according to Moore. The act of believing is only used in the secondary sense after what is believed in (fact) is true or false. If two persons say for instance: "I believe in God." The truth of their belief (sentence) is not in their respective acts of believing (sentence) according to him. The measure of the veracity of their beliefs is on God being true or false. And God in this case is the *proposition, meaning* or *fact* of their beliefs. It is on God being true that the truth of the beliefs of the two persons are based. In this light Moore writes: "Suppose a man believes that God exists; ... then to say that his belief is true seems to be exactly equivalent to saying that it *is a fact* that God exists or that God's existence is a fact."[147] The implication of this logic is that the difference between true and false belief is that a belief is true where what is believed is a fact, whereas a belief is false where what is believed is not a fact.[148] It means that a true belief or statement is the one in which there is in the universe a fact to which it corresponds, and vice versa.[149] Thus, subscribing to the correspondence theory of truth.

Russell is also an exponent of the correspondence theory of truth. Russell, in supporting the correspondence theory draws an epistemic illustration thus: "a cat is on a mat" is true if, and only if, there is in the world a cat and a mat, and the cat is related to the mat by virtue of being on

---

[147] George Edward Moore, *Some Main Problems in Philosophy* (New York: Allen. & Unwin, 1953), 250.
[148] Cf. Moore, *Some Main Problems in Philosophy,* 250.
[149] Cf. Moore, *Some Main Problems in Philosophy,* 277.

it. If any of the three pieces (the cat, the mat, and the relation between them which corresponds respectively to the subject, object, and verb of the statement) is missing, the statement is false.[150] This means that the truth of the statement consists in a correspondence of the statement or assertion with the fact, whereby the facts exist, and the belief is true. While presenting his *logical atomism* too, he tried to show how a true proposition and its corresponding fact share the same structure in the way the propositions *picture* the facts. And facts for Russell as in Wittgenstein are mind-independent realities. A true proposition is the one that corresponds with facts, while a false proposition is the one that bears a different correspondence to a fact (not necessarily the one that does not correspond to a fact).

Wittgenstein and John L. Austin subscribe to the correspondence theory of truth in their discourses. Wittgenstein argues that a statement can only be true, if it necessarily shares some structural isomorphism with the situation in the real world which makes it true. If this isomorphism of thought and reality are missing, a statement would be considered false. Austin on his part proposed that statements are truth bearers and states of affairs are truth makers, and for truth to be achieved, it must consist in the correlation of these two conditions. It is the correlation of two conventions: demonstrative convention (relating token state of affairs to statements) and descriptive convention (relating types of states of affairs to sentence types expressing those statements) that make truth achievable. Truth is the correspondence of statements to the state of affairs according to Austin, thus, agreeing to the fundamental position of the correspondence theory as

---

[150] Cf. Richard Kirkham, *Theories of Truth: A Critical Introduction* (Cambridge: MIT Press, 1992), section 4.3

captured by Eboh that: "Truth is the agreement between the statement of fact and actual fact or situation which the judgment claims to describe." [151] Hamlyn, in support, equally posits that: "a statement is true if and only if it corresponds with fact."[152] Judgment of a sentence is true if it attributes a character to the object which the object really possesses and it is false if it attributes a character to the object which the object does not possess.[153]

6.3 Criticism of the Correspondence Theory of Truth

Critics of correspondence theory of truth question the possibility of comparing and corresponding thoughts with reality, especially as thoughts are not easily known in their actual form. Eboh in this regard asks: "How can we compare ideas with reality? ... since we know only our experience, how can we get outside our ideas to reality as it actually is?" [154] Thoughts or ideas are obscure and not obvious, thus, knowing what is in the mind could become difficult before one can correspond it to reality, especially where truth rests in another person other than oneself. Related to that is the uncertainty or unreliability of reality in the correspondence theory as perceived by the senses. Given that our sense-data and even sense organs may not be accurate in their representations of the true nature of reality or perceptible experiences, corresponding our ideas to them or the objects of their perceptions may be erroneous. If one's ideas agree with a reality perceived erroneously, such agreement will be an agreement in error and not in truth.

---

[151] Eboh, *Theory of Knowledge*, 41.
[152] Hamlyn, *The Theory of Knowledge*, 116-117.
[153] Cf. Eboh, *Theory of Knowledge*, 41.
[154] Eboh, *Theory of Knowledge*, 45.

Thus, Eboh states that a major problem of the correspondence theory is that it assumes that "our sense-data are clear and accurate and that they discover the nature of the world just as it is."[155] This assumption is questioned according to Eboh, by the Idealists and Pragmatics who point out that:

> In perception the mind tends to enter into and modify our view of the world. If our powers of perception were diminished or increased or if we possessed fewer or more sense organs, the world might appear quite different, since we cannot know the object or event apart from our sense data. Hence, in their view, it is foolish to talk about whether or not our judgment corresponds with the thing as it is in itself.[156]

On another note, the theory is criticized on the ground that there are certain forms of truth which may not have obvious reality to which to correspond.

> We have knowledge of meaning (definition), relations, and values as in mathematics, logic, and ethics. Some of the ideas that we want to verify have no objects outside the area of human thought with which we can make comparisons and check for correspondence. The ideas in these areas are not just 'there in the world,' for example, the statement '2+2=4' is true and states a fact, but the fact in question cannot be said to be in the world in any obvious sense, though it does have objectivity.[157]

So, how does this theory account for some truths which could be certain by their intuition and values, but do not have any empirical or visible reality that correspond to them? To what do purely intuitive and speculative truths

---

[155] Eboh, *Theory of Knowledge*, 45.
[156] Eboh, *Theory of Knowledge*, 46.
[157] Eboh, *Theory of Knowledge*, 46.

correspond? One may agree that they are logical truths, but they are not logical facts. They are logical truths based on logical coherence of ideas and premises, but they do not have any obvious facts. And does this mean that logical truths are false? The same applies to mathematical truths which do not have obvious facts one can find out there in the world of experience or reality. The truth of mathematics is based on the theoretical methods like addition, subtraction, induction, deduction and so on. They are not derived from any concrete and obvious content or correspondence. How does correspondence theory account for such purely intellective truths which do not have material contents for obvious correspondence?

How about religious and moral truths like the idea of God, angels, heaven, hell, courage, virtue, and truth itself, which do not have obvious realities to correspond to? There are certainly religious truths that may not have visible or demonstrable existence, but which are believed with rational justifications to be true.[158] Would they be taken to be false because they do not have any physical realities that agree with them? The truth of God may lack empirical correspondence, but it can be demonstrated logically and morally as Aquinas did in his *Quinque viae* (Five Ways) of cosmological proof for the existence of God.[159] The same relates to moral truth. Where does one find an obvious correspondence to the virtue of truth itself, or other virtues like courage, honesty, integrity *et cetera*? One may have instances or illustrations of these, but certainly not a thing that represents them obviously or realistically as such. There

---

[158] Cf. Ani, *Introduction to Philosophy of History*, 162.
[159] Cf. Aquinas, *Summa Theologiae* Part 1, q. 2 a.3 and Humphrey Uchenna Ani, *Introducing Philosophy to a Lay-mind* (Enugu: Black Belt Konzult Ltd, 2008), 57.

is no obvious empirical thing called truth or courage. Thus, one may object to this theory because it is too narrow and reductionistic to only scientific or empirical proofs. It anchors only on truths of scientific domain, and fails to reflect the domains of morality, intuition, and religion, which have no obvious facts. It ignores the fact that reality involves religious and moral truths, even when there may not be religious or moral facts and data to which the religious and moral truths can correspond.

However, some of the responses by exponents of correspondence theory of truth on the issue of logical, moral, and religious truths which do not have obvious facts are that there are some other kinds of facts they correspond to. They claim that logical truths for instance correspond to facts about linguistic conventions; moral truths correspond to social-behavioral facts and religious truths correspond to faith-facts that may be more mysterious than obvious. In this case, one may not argue against the correspondence theory with the point that some truths do not have facts. What they may not have could be obvious facts, but they have facts of a different nature and kind.

On another note, some scholars like Frege have argued that since correspondence is based on concept-object relationship, what exists between them is not really an agreement of realistic relationship but a semantic relationship. The truth of their relationship may not rely so much on the identity of the object as it does on the semantic qualification of the relationship. If this is the case, then it is the logical correspondence expressed in words, and not the reality described, that carries the truth-value. Against this point is the response of some correspondence theorists that language or semantics only describe logical relationship of thoughts and things, and do not carry the truth of things and their relations to ideas. Their reason is that language has a lot of factors like sensation which affect its ability to accurately express the truth of a thing. Time, location, and convention in some cases may affect the true linguistic representation of reality. Take for instance where one reality is called "morning star" and "evening star" by language, using different names.[160] This is why sometimes a statement may correlate to an object or state of affairs in arbitrary linguistic conventions without mirroring the inner structures or real nature of its correlation. When this happens, the truth of the reality is lost or limited by linguistic conventions.

---

[160]The names "morning star" and "evening star" are misleading because they both refer to the same celestial object, Venus, which is not even a star but a planet (the second planet from the sun and close to the earth). It is the third brightest object in the sky from our perception on earth, behind the sun and the moon. Given its orbital movements, it may sometimes appear to be leading the sun and would be seen at dawn (prior to sunrise), thus called *morning star*. At some other time, it appears trailing the sun and would be seen at dusk (after sunset) and is called *evening star*. Thus, morning star and evening star actually refer to the same Venusian phenomenon changing movement at different times of twilight. Cf. David R. Williams, "Venus Fact Sheet," *NASA Goddard Space Flight Center*. Archived from the original on 11 May 2018. Retrieved 15 April 2021.

Chapter Seven: **The Coherence Theory of Truth**

7.1 Knowing What Coherence Theory Means

The coherence theory of truth argues that a position or proposition (bearer of truth-value) is true when it "coheres with specific set of propositions or sentences or beliefs which are conventionally and logically acceptable."[161] The truth of any true proposition consists in the truth of other propositions to which such an individual true proposition belongs. The logical representation asserts that:

(1) A proposition *p* is true,

(2) If and only if, *p* belongs to a system *S*,

(3) *S* is a coherent system (of truth).

A proposition is true if it coheres with the truths of other true propositions. Truth is that which is primarily consistent with and applicable to a broader body of conventionally or generally acceptable true propositions. If I say that I saw a 5 feet man who is black in color at the Bigard gate, it can be believed to be true and it might really be true. Its truth is based not only on its correspondence with reality but on the fact that the description fits properly into the general notion of the true height and color of what a human being looks like. By epistemic tradition of knowledge, human beings can be five feet tall and do have black colors too. But if I say that I saw a 20 feet man who is green in color with a long tail, it will be difficult to be believed or to be true. The reason for its falsity is that the description is inconsistent with the general and true idea of a normal human being by

---

[161] Ani, *Introduction to Philosophy of History*, 162.

epistemic standard and tradition. Human beings do not reach 20 feet in height. They are not green in color unless painted such and they do not have tails. This is to say that the veracity of a proposition or claim is based on its conformity with a verity system. Something or a proposition is true, if its claims agree with a body of truths related to it. Truth is rooted in the correlation of body of true propositions with each other, and not basically in correlation of propositions with reality.

Coherence theory of truth affirms that something is true if it belongs to a part of an earlier acceptable system of truth. This is part of the reason some schools of thought identify coherence theory of truth with "confirmation holism,"[162] given that its truth is derived from its conformity, coherence, and consistency with significant and sufficient features of a system of truth already known and acceptable.[163] Coherence theory of truth strongly argues that "truth is a reciprocally consistent system of propositions, each of which gets its truth from the whole system."[164] Coherence with reason and reality constitutes the essence of truth. According to this theory, a proposition or position is valid only if it is part of an existing system of accurate positions or propositions. The truth of a proposition is dependent on its epistemic coherence with a proposition that is true, and it is such that it is a necessary constituent of a systematically coherent whole. This whole upon which the truth depends must, however, be so interdependent that every element that forms part of it must necessitate and entail every other element.[165] Total truth would therefore be

---

[162] Willard Quine and J.S. Ullian, *The Web of Belief* (New York: Random House, 1978), Ch. viii.
[163] Cf. Ani, *Introduction to Philosophy of History*, 163.
[164] Eboh, *Theory of Knowledge*, 43.
[165] Cf. Ani, *Introduction to Philosophy of History*, 163.

a property solely of a unique coherent system, whereby every truth has a degree proportionate to how it fully approximates to the absolute truth.[166]

Robert Audi on coherence theory of truth writes that: "Its central idea expressed very broadly is that a true proposition is one that coheres appropriately with certain other propositions."[167] He further adds that "the theory might say that a true proposition is one which is fully justified by virtue of coherence with every other relevant justified proposition, where a justified proposition is, minimally, one that at least someone is (or anyway might be) justified in believing."[168] Some of the criteria on which one can find elements of coherence include memory, introspection, inference, experience, and things generally believed by others.[169] If what I know coheres with what I already knew but stored in my memory, my memory will form a criterion for me to believe such to be true. That I have memory of Milan where I have lived and experienced life could give me a strong ground that Milan exists if one says so, and that some of the things said about it are reasonably acceptable or believable. In this case, what I believe about Milan is coherent with my memory of Milan and experience of Milan.

The contents of my introspective conclusions could affirm what I believe to be true too. That I can accept certain logical propositions to be true or false is based on the fact that my sense of inner logic can justify it and what a new proposition offers coheres with my logical sense. The same

---

[166] Cf. *Dictionary of Philosophy*, s.v. "Coherence Theory of Truth."
[167] Robert Audi, *Epistemology-A Contemporary Introduction to the Theory of Knowledge* (London: Routledge, 1998), 240.
[168] Audi, Epistemology, 241.
[169] Cf. Audi, Epistemology, 241.

applies to issues I can accept or believe because they cohere with my inferential thinking. What many people believe to be true can also form my point of coherence. If many people believe that Nigeria is an insecure society for so many reasons, it might form my reason in accepting or believing that Nigeria is an insecure society, even before having sufficient ground (of some of the reasons the people posit as justifications) to substantiate my belief.

7.2 The Argument of Coherence Theory

The central argument of the coherence theory of truth is that truth is rooted in coherence with verity order of logic whereby truth is not based on the facts of reality as such but on harmony of position or judgement with all other true positions or judgements. Its veracity is mainly on what is reasonable, based on related judgements and not on evidence at hand. As Audi explains further: "the central idea underlying coherentism is that the justification (justifiedness) of a belief depends on its coherence with other beliefs."[170] And he adds that this often happens internally to the subject knower: "whatever coherence among beliefs is; it is an internal relation, in the sense that what it holds among beliefs is a matter of how those beliefs (including their propositional content which is intrinsic to them) are related to one another and not to anything outside one's system of beliefs such as one's personal experience."[171] This internal inclination of coherence theory argues for internalism and, as such, places the coherence of beliefs or truth on the subject. This is why the coherence theory of truth is equally pro-rationalism. Thus, the chief proponents

---

[170] Audi, *Epistemology,* 189.
[171] Audi, *Epistemology*, 194.

of this theory of truth are mainly rationalists and idealists like Leibniz, Spinoza, Kant, Fichte, Schlegel, Hegel, Blanshard, Nicholas Rescher, Bradley, McTaggart, and so on. They all subscribe to the idea that truth is dependent on reasonable agreement of a judgment with other reasonable judgements. Eboh commenting on this writes that:

> The proponents of this theory maintain that we cannot directly compare our ideas and judgments with the world as it is, and so for them, truth is the consistency or harmony of all our judgments. A judgment is true if it is consistent with other judgments that are accepted as true. Hence, true judgments are those logically coherent with relevant judgments.[172]

In the light of this theory, one would hold a statement to be true if it fits into what is already known to be true or have happened, or agrees with what, from our past experience, one may reasonably expect to happen.[173] If for instance I say that 2+2=4, it is consistent with other true mathematical propositions in the system of addition that I have known like 4+4=8, 6+6+6=18 etc. But if I say that 3+3+3=1, that will be absurd and logically considered false in the system of mathematical logic. This is why the notion of Trinitarian formula of Three Persons in One God (1-Father+1-Son+1 Spirit=1 God) is absurd to both philosophical mentality and mathematical method. It is rather a truth acceptable and believed within Christian Theology and revealed mystery. The truth of the Three Persons in One God in the Christian belief (of the Blessed Trinity) is a case of theological Revealed True Belief (RTB), and not of the philosophical Justified True Belief (JTB). It is not a truth based on coherence with conventional

---

[172] Eboh, *Theory of Knowledge*, 42.
[173] Cf. Eboh, *Theory of Knowledge*, 42.

mathematical logic of addition. It is also not consistent with any system of truths seen in normal human experiences.

However, coherence theory of truth does not imply that one rejects innovative ideas or facts that may not have been experienced or is inconsistent with usual truth system without careful examination. Sometimes, even when we may resist certain new facts and ideas, they will be so obvious that rejecting them will be absurd and may even be tantamount to obscurantism. New facts and ideas may in some cases impose themselves against our earlier known facts and ideas and, as such, become imperative for us to accept, thereby altering our previous positions and arguments. As William James observes in his pragmatism, in the face of some facts or ideas: "a new theory is attacked as absurd; then it is admitted being true, but obvious and insignificant; finally, it is seen to be so important that its adversaries claim that they themselves discovered it."[174] Things that could have been considered absurd years back have also become normal experiences of truth today.

Maybe three thousand years ago, the earth was known to be flat while the sun revolved around it (*geocentrism*). Years later, it was found out that the earth is spherical and rather revolves round the sun in elliptical orbit (*heliocentrism*).[175] The truth about the earth in this logic is based on new insight and not really on the coherence of the

---

[174] William James, "Pragmatism's Conception of Truth," in Samuel Enoch Stumpf & James Fieser, *Philosophy, History and Problems, Seventh Edition* (New York: McGraw-Hill, 2008), 220.

[175] Cf. Nicholas Copernicus, *On the Revolutions of the Celestial Spheres*, cited by Jostein Gaarder, *Sophie's World, A Novel About the History of Philosophy,* ed. Paulette Moller (New York: Berkley Books, 1991), 204.

new insight with a system of astronomical truth known earlier.

Furthermore, if one claimed to be talking and seeing another person in China from Nigeria three hundred years ago, his claim could be considered false and absurd. This is because such a claim then was inconsistent with a possible or general true system of communication. But with the cell phone and digital culture in our Twenty-first Century, such a claim is as true as obvious beyond any empirical or rational doubt. The truth of talking and seeing someone in China from Nigeria through the video calls of so many media outlets in the Twenty-first Century has become obvious that its veracity defies doubt of fact or reason. The online virtual communication system has made new truths cancel old disbeliefs and claims which could not have been true three hundred years ago. As Eboh captures it: "occasionally, new facts or ideas will force themselves upon us and impress us so strongly with their truth that we need to service many of our previous conceptions, if not a whole system of thought."[176]

Eboh made a distinction of two forms of coherence theory of truth. He writes that "it is perhaps necessary to distinguish between the simple form of coherence theory and the enlarged form of the theory."[177] In the "simple form," there is restricted consideration of the consistency of a proposition or judgement within a specific system of truth or judgments. He explains that:

> The simple form simply demands an inner or formal consistency in the particular system *under consideration*, quite apart from any interpretation of the universe as a

---

[176] Eboh, *Theory of Knowledge*, 42.
[177] Eboh, *Theory of Knowledge*, 42.

whole. For example, in mathematics, assuming certain definitions and axioms, we can build up the systems of geometry implied by the definitions and axioms consistent with them. This system is then accepted as true because of the principle of consistency or logical implication. This is true of any other science or organized body of knowledge.[178]

The simple form of coherence theory of truth demands some internal formal consistency within a limited order like one where mathematical truth must respect the basic features expected of a mathematical logic and form to be true.[179] The simple form of coherence theory has equally been identified as the pure form of coherence theory by some epistemologists.

On a different note, the "enlarged form" of coherence theory is the one that involves an all-inclusive and self-consistent whole of reality. It has also been identified as mixed coherence theory by epistemologists. This means that the veracity of every true proposition, every true judgement and every practical truth system must be continuous with the whole reality and derive its meaning from the whole. Something is true according to this form if it agrees to a wider and generally accepted notion or belief of true propositions, true practices, and true judgments. This form of coherence is identified with the idealistic principle of consistency, according to Eboh, whereby truth is a reciprocally consistent system of propositions, and where each proposition gets its truth from the universal system of truth. He writes in this light that "in the idealist's view, it is the consistency of one human belief with that whole which makes them true when they are true. Thus, purely formal

---

[178] Eboh, *Theory of Knowledge*, 42-43.
[179] Cf. Ani, *Introduction to Philosophy of History*, 164.

consistency is abandoned and coherence with reality is made the essence of truth."[180]

What this stance is saying is that all we can do to get at the truth is to compare one judgment or set of judgments with others which are true, and if it is consistent with others, then it is obvious and rational that it must be true. It demands respecting the larger form or conventional nature of beliefs or acceptable conditions for something to be true.[181] If one says that Mr. Ngene has four legs, it is inconsistent with the wider or general idea of human description, and as such cannot be acceptable to be true. Therefore, the truth about Mr. Ngene must agree with the truth of the features and other descriptions of the human person, as generally or conventionally known to be true. It is the wider reality or the whole of reality that shapes the truth of every particular position, judgment, and practice that is true. Every truth system is continuous with the whole of reality of truth and derives its meaning from that that whole.[182] The supposition here is that every truth is partial and relative and can only be complete and correct when it fits into or tallies with the whole reality of other truths. The implication being that absolute truth is impossible, and that truth can only be partial. And if truth is partial, then a proposition or belief is true to the degree that it coheres with the whole true propositions or other beliefs that are true. Thus, we can only talk of degrees of truth of any proposition or belief in relation to wholeness (fullness) of truth which is merely rationalistic and not realistic.

---

[180] Eboh, *Theory of Knowledge*, 43.
[181] Cf. Ani, *Introduction to Philosophy of History*, 164.
[182] Cf. Eboh, *Theory of Knowledge*, 43.

7.3 Criticism of the Coherence Theory

The criticism of coherence theory of truth is strongly hinged on its rationalistic complications. The idea of coherence sometimes is vague and complicated in its implications. If consistency with a specified set of propositions is the ground for truth, what happens where two or more propositions which are inconsistent with themselves are consistent with a specified set of propositions? There may be a case in which two propositions may be consistent with a set of propositions but are not consistent with each other. When such happens, simple consistency would not be satisfactory to make a proposition true and, as such, truth becomes impossible to achieve. What this means is that consistency of a proposition is not sufficient to qualify a true proposition. Furthermore, a proposition might be consistent without being realistic. If one tells an arbitrary fairy tale which is consistent and constructed with no contradiction in its logical narrative, would it qualify such a tale to be considered true as one would take a historical truth that is based on true reports and facts? If consistency is made the measure of truth, so many fantastical and fictitious stories which do not have logical contradictions in their narratives would be true (even when they are not realistic, justifiable, or historically verifiable).[183]

Sometimes coherence can also be ambiguous in context and meaning. In some cases, it might mean simple consistency with a specified set of propositions. In other cases, it might involve entailment. By entailment, a proposition would be consistent with a set of specified propositions if, and only if, it is entailed by members of such

---

[183] Cf. Bertrand Russell, *Philosophical Essays* (London: Longmans, Green and Company, 1910), 215-216.

a specified set. Sometimes the applications of coherence as either simple consistency or entailment can bring some confusion in the examination of truth based on coherence theory. Entailment is stronger than simple consistency in terms of what coherence may imply in the logical relationship of propositions. If the logic of addition says that 1+1=2 by mathematical entailment, what happens in a context where the same law of addition is applied in a moral sense whereby there is no mathematical entailment but simple moral consistency? If 1+1=2 in mathematics, 1+1=1 could also be coherent by simple moral consistency and relationship understanding of marital logic. This is seen where two people are meant to think and act as one in respect of mutual moral unity and oneness of purpose in love.

As the popular saying goes: "1+1=1 in marriage mathematics". If this stance is understood and believed to be true by many, as a social or moral truth, it will be considered true in its context and widely acclaimed value. By the theory of coherence, if many people believe the set of propositions that 1+1=1 in marriage is true or that 1+1+1=1 is true in the Christian Theology of the nature of the Three Persons in One God (of the Blessed Trinity), my personal belief in these *truly* held propositions would be considered true, given that it coheres with the set of beliefs widely accepted and shared by many to be true. But will this coherence make any of the propositions logically and mathematically true in themselves outside the majoritarian ground? Will 1+1+1 entail 1 (and not 3), or is 1+1+1=1 true because it is consistent with held true belief in the Trinitarian formular?

Another criticism associated with the coherence theory of truth is that "it could lead to a dangerous circularity in which we have a number of false statements, each of which claims to be true because it is consistent with the others."[184] Coherence theory of truth often does not distinguish between consistent truth and consistent error. Thus, if the theory bases its truth on the consistency of a proposition with a set of beliefs or acceptable logic, one can argue that it is possible that a negative or false proposition or set of beliefs could be consistent with earlier acceptable set of false beliefs, which therefore will justify them. This will be tantamount to truth based on consistent falsity, which in truth is no truth. Consistent error, no matter how long it might last, can never amount to truth.

It is absurd and contradictory to the logic of veracity to assume that something or a proposition becomes true by being consistent with a widely accepted error in the past or an error accepted by a majority or convention. A situation whereby veracity of propositions is measured by majority stance on what ought to be true is tantamount to the reduction of veracity to uncritical epistemic majoritarianism. A case in which consistency with a conventional or traditional error rooted in ignorance or lack of insight is used to gauge the truth of a proposition is inconsistent and incongruous with the real content of truth. Is popularity of an idea equivalent to its veracity? What happens when a collective and rationally consistent proposition is bereft of factual consistency with reality? Does the longevity of error make it right? Have there not been instances where held beliefs have been erroneous for centuries?

In a related point, a third case against this theory is that its circularity system can lead to epistemic infinite

---

[184] Eboh, *Theory of Knowledge*, 46.

regression. If one needs another or other beliefs to justify/cohere with what one holds to be true, those beliefs will also need other ones to be justified or be cohered to (to be true), otherwise they would not be reliable criteria for belief. Even the beliefs they need to be justified would need other beliefs to justify them (that is, other beliefs on which to cohere). It will then be such that every belief will need the next belief to be believed in. Thus, leading to infinite regress.

Still, how if the beliefs a particular belief needs to cohere are partially untrue or false? And how if the belief one needs to cohere with or be consistent with is relative? If what I believe to be true is a relative truth emanating from a person, does it not make my truth relative, too, by its coherence with a relative truth? A statement may cohere with a person's belief system and end up being true only on the relative criterion of the person on whom their truth is based. The same goes for where a person's belief is based on or coheres with another society's relative tradition or culture. So, what happens if the relative culture or tradition one or another coheres with is not true? In this case, one's belief must depend on the falsity or the relative truth of another culture or tradition to be true. Thus, rendering the belief or truth logically, ultimately, false, and relative.

The fourth case against the coherence theory of truth is that it ignores factual consistency. It is mainly dealing with logical and semantic relationships of propositions without engaging the facts associated with them. This is why many have considered it to be over steeped in facile intellectualism and rationalism sans facts. As Eboh notes, coherence theory of truth "fails to furnish an adequate test for the judgement of everyday experience. If the test of coherence is used, then it needs to be stated more with reference to factual consistency, that is, the agreement between a judgement and a definite environmental situation."[185]

There is no doubt that a new fact which is so obvious and true, and at the same time does not cohere with any known or previous set of beliefs could emerge. In such a case, will such an obvious fact be denied or be rejected because it does not cohere with any known truth or previous set of beliefs? If coherence takes this extreme measure, it can only block any epistemic progress, empirical innovation or factual discoveries that may emerge. A proposition can be true even though it does not cohere with any known truth or set of beliefs.

On another note, some scholars like Paul Thagard have argued that coherence theory has given the mind too many powers in determining the truth, against the mind-independent world which should rather be the measure of truth. According to him, if history shows that there is a mind-independent world, the aim of representations by beliefs and other truth bearers should be to describe or affirm this world, and not to determine its truth by relating other representations to each other. In this argument, one understands that what we call true propositions or set of beliefs are representations of a mind-independent reality. So, when we talk about the truth of a set of beliefs as the criterion for truth, it is logically derived from the mind-independent realities whose veracity they represent. Consequently, it is this mind-independent reality which ultimately validates the veracity of truths contained in the true set of propositions of coherence theory. In this case, it is the correspondence of the propositions to reality that

---

[185] Eboh, *Theory of Knowledge*, 47.

determines truth (correspondence theory of truth), and not the truth of the propositions in themselves. The set of beliefs with which other true propositions cohere are truths of some realities they represent.

Besides, there are some self-presenting states like what one feels and even self-evident truths that do not need to cohere with any system of truth to be true. If I feel pain, the truth of my pain does not need to cohere with any system of truth to be true. And if one says that boys are young men, it is such self-evident that no criteria or coherence with any system of truth will be required to validate it. In some extrasensory perceptions like mystical experiences, coherence might be otiose to determine their veracity. But strong exponents of coherence theory will still argue that even such forms of truth are still dependent, in some way, on the experiences or judgements of the past to be identified and be confirmed as truth. They posit that if I feel pain, then I know that what I am feeling is pain and not something else because I have previous pains consistent with my current pain. If one says boys are young men, it belongs to a set of previous education on the classes of people in the society, to which the self-evident knowledge of "boys are young men" belong. And even the extrasensory perceptions are true because they fall into the forms of other extrasensory experiences that can sometimes be seen in some spiritual or religious experiences. However, in the face of the criticisms and factual emptiness or other lapses of the correspondence and coherence theories of truth, there is another major truth theory called the pragmatic theory of truth.

Chapter Eight: The Pragmatic Theory of Truth

8.1 Knowing What Pragmatism Is

The pragmatic theory of truth according to Eboh argues that "the test of truth is utility, workability, or satisfactory results. There is no such thing as static or absolute truth. Truth is redefined to mean something that happens to a judgment or an idea."[186] The central position of this theory is that something is true if it works out in practice and, or if it leads to useful or practical results.[187] One of the advocates of this theory, William James writes that: "True ideas are those that we can assimilate, validate, corroborate and verify; false ideas are those that we cannot."[188] This is to underline the fact that truth is rooted in expediency, whereby something is true because it is effective and useful when applied to actual practice. The test of truth is shown in how it works in practice and application. The proponents of this theory reject the correspondence theory because it identifies truth with only experience, even when it is useless, and equally reject the coherent theory because it is too formalistic and rationalistic. They rather opt for a notion of truth that is more practical and useful where:

(1) A proposition p is true,

(2) If and only if p is W,

(3) W is what works.

---

[186] Eboh, *Theory of Knowledge*, 44.
[187] Cf. Ani, *Introduction to Philosophy of History*, 166.
[188] William James, "Pragmatism's Conception of Truth," in *Essays in Pragmatism*, ed. Alburey Castell (New York: Hafner Press, 1975), 160.

They hold that a proposition is true if it is useful to believe. According to Omoregbe, it "holds that a statement or theory is true if it works in practice. An idea is true if it works and leads to beneficial results."[189] Pragmatism as a system of philosophy does not accept that we can know anything outside the things that help us to attend to human problems. This is why they claim that metaphysical and idealistic realities like substances, essences, ultimate and spiritual realities, (if they do not serve useful need), do not exist and as such, there is no truth in believing them.

Pragmatists are often against authoritarianism, intellectualism, and rationalism where these idealistic and spiritual stances are accepted, defended, or justified without useful objective. The only condition that may make a pragmatist believe in the truth of these entities is where believing them can serve as solutions or working concepts for practical issues. "For the pragmatist, an idea or a theory or a hypothesis is true if it works out in practice, if it leads to satisfactory results."[190] Being useful, for them, is an essential mark of truth, and beliefs that lead to the best use in our actions (or guide our actions effectively) and promote success are the most justified beliefs. To understand the stance of the pragmatic theory of truth, it is important to reference the idea of pragmatism as a philosophical movement and its development in the history of philosophy.

According to Stumpf and Fieser, "Pragmatism emerged at the end of the Nineteenth Century as the most original contribution of American thought to the enterprise of philosophy."[191] The key ideas of pragmatism originated

---

[189] Omoregbe, *Epistemology*, 43.
[190] Eboh, *Theory of Knowledge*, 45.
[191] Samuel Enoch Stumpf and James Fieser, *Philosophy, History and Problems*, Seventh Edition (New York: McGraw-Hill, 2008), 371.

in 1870s, at the so called "Metaphysical Club"–a conversational philosophical club that met in Cambridge, Massachusetts, comprising of eminent scholars, philosophers, psychologists and so on. This conversational club examined and rejected radical foundationalism of Western metaphysics. The club was formed in January 1872 and was dissolved in December of the same year, 1872. The club, according to Charles Sanders Peirce, was named half-ironically because it was not to promote but to demote metaphysical discourses.[192] It was formed to reject radical foundationalist metaphysics in favor of moderate foundationalism, where critical thinking of a pragmatist and positivist nature will be pursued.[193] It was eventually within the philosophical discussions in this club that pragmatism as system and movement in philosophy was born.[194] The information about this club was mentioned by Peirce who participated in it with the philosopher and psychologist, William James. Writing on pragmatism, Stumpf and Fieser remark that:

> The movement received its theoretical formulation by Charles S. Peirce (1839-1914). It enjoyed wide and popular circulation through the brilliant and lucid essays of William James (1842-1910). It was then methodically implemented into daily affairs of American institutions by John Dewey (1859-1952). The central message of these three philosophers is that there is little value in philosophical theories that do not somehow make a difference in daily life. Pragmatism was more of a

---

[192] Cf. Charles S. Peirce, *The Philosophy of Peirce, Selected Writings*, ed. Justus Buchler (Harcourt: Brace and Company,1960), 269.
[193] Cf. Louis Menand, *The Metaphysical Club: A Story of Ideas in America* (New York: Farrar, Straus and Giroux, 2002), 226.
[194] Cf. Charles. S. Peirce, "The Founding of Pragmatism," *The Hound and Horn: A Harvard Miscellany* v. II, no. 3 (1929): 284.

method of solving problems than it was a metaphysical system of the world.[195]

Charles Sanders Peirce, William James and John Dewey are very much linked with this theory, and this is why their positions would be used later to demonstrate the pragmatic theory of truth. Peirce is known for being the first to propose the pragmatic theory of truth as a belief that will withstand future scrutiny. James has the credit for popularizing the theory as the most dependable and useful true belief. Dewey is known for having reframed the concept and renamed it "Instrumentalism." He made it more assertive in contemporary epistemology, history, and education. The tenets of pragmatism were initially propagated and promoted by Peirce and James. Later, the inspirations and details of the ideas of the system were carried on by John Dewey, whose philosophy is another version of pragmatism called Instrumentalism.

Pragmatism was instituted as a mediation between two rival trends of thought in the Nineteenth Century.[196] There was a trend inspired by empiricism, utilitarianism and materialism which promoted mechanism of the human person, through the natural sciences as seen in the Darwinian biologism. They tend to see reality as an assembly of parts and as such evaluate them in their parts or individuality. There is also the opposing trend that favored vitalism and human-centred traditions as inspired by forms of rationalism and idealism seen in the works of philosophers like Plato, Descartes, Kant, and Hegel. They tend to see reality in their holistic order, and as such used the common principles of this order in their evaluation of

---

[195] Stumpf and Fieser, *Philosophy, History and Problems*, 317.
[196] Cf. Stumpf and Fieser, *Philosophy, History and Problems*, 371.

things. Like the empiricists and the mechanists, pragmatists try to see things from their perspectives without judging them entirely. And like the vitalists and idealists, they equally value structures of holism and tradition as morality and religion in as much as they contribute to the human purpose.[197]

Thus, the three principal exponents of pragmatism (Peirce, James, and Dewey) took to different versions of the movement, harnessing and representing different angles of its meaning. Peirce delved more on logic and science, James dwelt on psychology and religion, while Dewey dealt with themes on education, ethics, and sociology.[198] The spread of pragmatism came through the lectures and publications of these three skilled academicians. Peirce and James embarked on publications and lectures between the 1870s and 1900s to push the concept and tenets of pragmatism forward. They formulated theories and methods to identify empty disputes, principles, methods, and maxims which they classified as false and useless if they do not address practical human situations. Such principles and theories, according to them, are often found within metaphysical foundationalism of philosophy. To explore the essential points of the pragmatic theory of truth, we shall look at the pragmatism and theories of truth associated with each of these pillars of pragmatism: Peirce, James, and Dewey.

8.2 The Pragmatic Theory of Truth in Peirce

Peirce's pragmatic theory of truth is derived from his pragmatic theory of meaning. Peirce "coined the word

---

[197] Cf. Stumpf and Fieser, *Philosophy, History and Problems*, 372.
[198] Cf. Stumpf and Fieser, *Philosophy, History and Problems*, 372.

pragma (meaning 'act' or 'deed') to emphasize the fact that words derive their meanings from actions of some sort. Our deeds are clear and distinct only when we can translate them into some type of operation."[199] He believes that the meaning of truth lies on its "practical bearings." He argues that the difference between describing a belief as true and other related attributes like creativity is that it has practical effect. He gives examples with the truth about the words "hard" and "heavy," saying that they have meaning only because of the practical effects associated with the terms. According to Stumpf and Fieser:

> Thus, hard means that which cannot be scratched by many other substances, and heavy means that which will fall if we let go of it. Underscoring the decisive role of effects in the meanings of words, Peirce argues that there would be no difference between a challenging thing and a soft thing if they did not test differently. From such simple examples Peirce generalized about the nature of meaning and knowledge. His basic point was that 'our idea of anything is our idea of its sensible effects.'[200]

For him, words have no meaning if they refer to objects about which no practical effects can be conceived. Peirce very much adheres to scientific languages too, to achieve his demand for empirical and practical justification of truth. He is critical of rationalist theories like the coherence theory of truth because they based their validity of truth on consistency between ideas, with no reference to practical or external effects. In Cartesianism for instance, Peirce sees a truth based only on clear and distinct ideas grasped by intuition and which has no environmental circumstances upon which it can be justified. Such ground

---

[199] Stumpf and Fieser, *Philosophy, History and Problems*, 373.
[200] Stumpf and Fieser, *Philosophy, History and Problems*, 373.

of truth according to him is mere intellectualism isolated from the real criteria of truth as found in practical effects. For him, "We derive meanings not through intuition but by experience or experiment. Thus, meanings are not individual or private but social and public."[201] The problem with truth based only on private isolationism is that there is no way of testing such claims or ideas by their effects or public consequences.

Discussing belief in relation to truth and certainty, he argues that beliefs stand in-between thought and action, and this is where they guide our desires and shape our actions. However, beliefs are 'unfixed' by doubts, and when this happens, thoughts are employed to assist beliefs overcome doubts to attain truth. We fix our beliefs with thought when rattled by doubt to attain truth. And when we attain this fixed point of belief, Peirce posits that there are three main methods through which we can retain our certainty.

The first is by tenacity, "whereby people cling to beliefs, refusing to entertain doubts about them or to consider arguments or evidence for another view."[202] The second means is authority, whereby people under authority are required to accept certain ideas or beliefs under threat of punishment. The third is by philosophical reason whereby people settle questions and accept certain positions as true because they agree to reason as seen in the works of Plato, Descartes, and Hegel. Later, he disagrees with these three methods of truth because none relates to experience and operational behavior. He opted for a fourth option which is the scientific method. In his argument:

---

[201] Stumpf and Fieser, *Philosophy, History and Problems*, 373.
[202] Stumpf and Fieser, *Philosophy, History and Problems*, 374.

The method of science, by contrast, is built on the assumption that there are real things, things that are entirely independent of our opinions about them. Moreover, because these real things affect our senses according to regular laws, we can assume that they will affect each observer the same way. Beliefs that are grounded in real things can, therefore, be verified, and their 'fixation' can be a public act rather than a private one.[203]

Scientific method therefore is superior in the justification of truth for Peirce than the other three methods. It is not rooted in irrationality as seen in tenacity, precludes fear as in authority, and it is not fixed in empty rationalism as in philosophical reason. For the pragmatic theory of truth of Peirce, "the method of science requires that we state not only what truth we believe but also how we arrived at it."[204] Furthermore, the procedure of the scientific method of truth is available for anyone who has interest in engaging it. This is why it is not individualistic as in Cartesian intellectualism and as such open for public or community verifiability and examination. It is also self-critical by constantly subjecting its conclusions to constant tests and adjustments based on new evidence or insights. And given its open approach to truth, it encourages cooperation among all members of the scientific community to be engaged in the truth project. "Such cooperation prevents any individual or group from shaping truth to fit its own interests. Conclusions of science, then, must be conclusions that all scientists can draw. Similarly, in questions of belief and truth, it should be possible for anyone to come to the same conclusions."[205]

---

[203] Stumpf and Fieser, *Philosophy, History and Problems*, 374.
[204] Stumpf and Fieser, *Philosophy, History and Problems*, 374.
[205] Stumpf and Fieser, *Philosophy, History and Problems*, 374.

This might not imply that there may not be disagreement in the scientific community. There may be antagonistic views, but the progress of investigation carries these divergent views by a force outside of themselves to the same conclusion which will be true. This force, according to Peirce, is embodied in the conception of truth and reality. The truth is that opinion which is fated to be ultimately agreed to by all who investigate, and the object represented in this opinion is real.

      He further holds that all the followers of science are fully persuaded that the processes of investigation in scientific methods are practical, reliable, and fallible too. And if spurred enough, they will give reliable solutions to every question to which their methods can be applied. The conclusion which is "fated" to be ultimately agreed to by all who investigate is what he meant by truth. By fate here, he does not mean that determined by superstition but that which is sure to come true and can no longer be avoided. What this means is that truth is a product of scientific investigation and consensus. Truth is a fruit of scientific inquiry if scientific inquiry is allowed freely and indefinitely. Truth is that agreement of an abstract statement with the ideal limit towards which endless investigation would tend to bring scientific belief. Truth is therefore not dependent on unanimity or actual end of inquiry but is an effect of an inquiry pushed to its ultimate and indefeasible end. This is different from weak inquiries and affirmations as it may be associated with several forms of cognitive bias. True belief is one that has and will continue to hold up to sustained inquiry and examination. In practical terms, to have a true belief is to have a belief that is dependable in the face of all future challenges.

Truth is measured by its dependability, by its scientific faith and its ability to be endorsed and be adopted as a basis for action. But this does not imply that the truth must be accurate always. The concordance of abstract statement with ideal limit towards endless investigation for scientific belief and as such, the truth, may possess inaccuracy and one-sidedness while still constituting its essential ingredients. Peirce's pragmatic theory of truth accommodates approximation, incompleteness, and partiality in truth, which is otherwise called *fallibilism* in pragmatic philosophy.

On another note, the emphasis of Peirce on practical dimension of true beliefs is a deliberate attempt to play down the significance of theoretical questions on truth and the coherence theory of truth in particular. Though leaning on experiential or operational correspondence as a criterion of truth, this theory is still skeptical of the correspondence theory of truth since it does not shed light on what makes true beliefs valuable. For Peirce, the importance of truth rests not on conceptual connection between beliefs and reality, but on the practical connection between doubt and belief. And where our beliefs can no longer be doubted and nothing upon it can be improved with any further evidence or new insight, one can then conclude that one has arrived at the truth.

8.3 The Pragmatic Theory of Truth in James

James is credited with the popularization of the pragmatic theory of truth. In his series of lectures and articles, he offers an account of truth like Peirce that is rooted in the practical role of the concept. Unlike Peirce who fixed truth on indefeasibility and unassailability, James holds that the essence of truth is in its satisfaction. True beliefs according to him are satisfying beliefs. In his 1907 lectures published as *Pragmatism: A New Name for Some Old Ways of Thinking*, he argues that ideas become true as far as they help us get into satisfactory relations with other parts of our experience. True ideas for him are like tools, and as such they make us more efficient by helping us do what needs to be done. Truth is also utilitarian because any idea upon which we can ride, any idea upon which we can prosper from one experience to any other part, linking things satisfactorily, working securely, simplifying, saving labor, is true for that much. In his article, *Pragmatism's Conception of Truth* as cited by Stumpf and Fieser, truth is instrumental when,

> Agreement thus turns out to be essentially an affair of leading that is useful because it is in quarters that contain objects that are important. True ideas lead us into useful verbal and conceptual quarters and up to useful sensible termini. They lead to consistency, stability, and flowing human intercourse. They lead away from eccentricity and isolation, from foiled and barren thinking.[206]

James credits the utilitarian concept of truth to Dewey, but he equally endorses that too. One must consider the pragmatic "cash-value" of an idea or thing to understand its truth. True beliefs are primarily useful and dependable. In pragmatic logic, something is either true because it is useful, or it is useful because it is true. The basic pragmatic questions in the quest for truth include: What concrete difference will an idea bring into anyone's actual life? "How will truth be realized? What experiences will be different from those which would obtain if the belief were false? What, in short, is the truth's cash value in experiential

---

[206] Stumpf and Fieser, *Philosophy, History and Problems*, 226.

terms?"[207] These basic questions will lead to answers in which truth is that which we can assimilate, validate, corroborate, and verify. Falsity will be the opposite. True beliefs are the ones that enable us to make accurate judgments and predictions of actual situations, and which contribute to values of our concrete lives. This is why the idea of God is true in pragmatism if it yields religious comfort and contributes to our happiness and fulfilment. The true belief is whatever proves itself to be good, useful, effective, and expedient in any fashion. But what happens where there is useless truth or where there is useful falsehood? No doubt, there are certain truths that do not have practical values, and there are falsehoods that may have practical values. Lies can sometimes be told to avoid a greater danger or even to build harmony in relationships.

James' pragmatism tries to unite the basic tenets of the correspondence and coherence theories of truth. It propounds that truth must be verified in such a way that thoughts and statements have to correspond to actual things and that they have to cohere together as can be verified in observed results of the application of an idea to actual practice.[208] Truth according to James carries the essential elements of the two theories and expresses them in practice.[209] In relation to coherence theory, truth must agree with verified results that already exist in actual realties, and as correspondence, he says that "all true processes must lead to the face of directly verifying sensible experiences

---

[207] Stumpf and Fieser, *Philosophy, History and Problems*, 222.
[208] Cf. Encyclopedia of Philosophy, Vol.6, s.v. "Pragmatic Theory of Truth,"
[209] Cf. William James, "The Thing and its Relations," *Essays in Radical Empiricism,* ed. William James (New York: Longman, Green and Co, 1912), 100.

somewhere, which somebody's ideas have copied."[210] However, admission of these contributive elements from these two theories of truth does not rule out his criticisms against them.

Against the coherence theory of truth as cited by Stumpf and Fieser, James argues that:

> The value of any theory rests in its capacity to solve problems, and not in its internal verbal consistency. Instead of mere consistency, James writes, we 'must bring out of each word its practical cash value'-that is, we must focus on results. When we find a theory that does not make a difference one way or another for practical life, then the theory is meaningless, and we should abandon it.[211]

And against the correspondence theory of truth, Stumpf and Fieser explain that James rejects the correspondence theory of truth because it assumes that an idea copies reality, and an idea is, therefore, true if it copies what is 'out there' accurately.[212] In their explanations on the stance of James on this theory:

> Truth means essentially an inert static relation. When you have your true idea of anything, there is an end to the matter. You are in possession, you know. But the truth, according to James, is less fixed than this. Like the theory of meaning, truth involves asking, 'What concrete difference will its being true make in anyone's actual life'.[213]

---

[210] William James, "Lecture 6: Pragmatism's Conception of Truth," in *Pragmatism: A New Name for Some Old Ways of Thinking,* ed. William James (New York: Longman, Green and Co.1907), 83.
[211] Stumpf and Fieser, *Philosophy, History and Problems*, 376.
[212] Cf. Stumpf and Fieser, *Philosophy, History and Problems*, 376.
[213] Stumpf and Fieser, *Philosophy, History and Problems*, 376.

To underline the pragmatic criterion of truth, James draws an illustration with a clock on a wall, which we take to be a clock, not because we have a "copy view" of it but because of its internal mechanism which we cannot see, and which provides us services. As cited in Stumpf and Fieser:

> Our idea of the clock consists mainly of its face and hands, which in no way matches 'reality.' Still, our limited idea of the clock passes for true because we *use* this conception as a clock, and as such it *works*. Some practical consequences of this idea are that we can go to work 'on time' and catch the train.[214]

Thus, "ideas become true as far as they help us make successful connections among various parts of our experience. Truth, is therefore, part of the process of living."[215] It is success and functionality that define truth according to James. It is neither the objective presence or copy-view of reality as in correspondence theory nor internal coherence of a mechanism as in coherent theory of truth. He believes that basing truth on what works will help to resolve disputes and polemics in philosophy. We must measure the veracity of whatever we claim to know by how it works or bears practical impact. When some disputes become irresolvable, James would ask: Which theory fits the facts and functions well in real life? When that is found, then it is the true theory.[216]

James, sequel to his belief in pragmatic functionality extends and expands his scope of truth beyond scientific verifiability to the realm of the mystical, for as long as such a belief works. He writes: "On pragmatic principles, if the

---

[214] Stumpf and Fieser, *Philosophy, History and Problems*, 376.
[215] Stumpf and Fieser, *Philosophy, History and Problems*, 376.
[216] Cf. Stumpf and Fieser, *Philosophy, History and Problems*, 377.

hypothesis of God works satisfactorily in the widest sense of the word, then it is 'true.'"[217] It is the absence of this pragmatic method that sometimes leads to disputes among philosophers. He writes:

> Truth, as any dictionary will tell you, is a property of certainty of our ideas. It means their 'agreement', as falsity means disagreement, with 'reality'. Pragmatists and intellectualists both accept this definition as a matter of course. They begin to quarrel only after the question is raised as to what may precisely be meant by the term 'agreement', and what by the term 'reality', when reality is taken as something for our ideas to agree with.[218]

According to James, pragmatism should be adopted as a method and theory of truth rather than wasting efforts on discerning truth between contrasting schools of thought. Efforts in philosophy should be used to consider the pragmatic 'cash-value' of having true beliefs and the practical differences of having true ideas.[219] By the term 'cash-value,' he means the practical consequences that come from discerning the truth behind arguments, through the pragmatic method. Beliefs are not static or fixed, they are mutable and dynamic, and this is because they are true depending on their utility in a person's specific situation. As problems change, so will the most useful way to solve a problem shift, and so does the property of truth. Thus, beliefs are true at one time but false at another and can be true for one person but false for another. This implies that pragmatic truth can be flexible or relative.

---

[217] William James, "Lecture 8: Pragmatism and Religion," in *Pragmatism: A New Name for Some Old Ways of Thinking,* 105.
[218] James, *"Pragmatism's Conception of Truth,"* 76ff.
[219] Cf. John Capps, "A Common-Sense Pragmatic Theory of Truth," in *Philosophia,* 48, no. 2 (2020): 463.

Furthermore, in his lectures on "*Pragmatism: A New Name for Some Old Ways of Thinking*" in 1907, James identifies what he called '*The Present Dilemma in Philosophy*' on truth. He identifies what he saw as a fundamental and irresoluble clash between two ways of thinking, which he promises pragmatism would overcome. He observes that the history of philosophy is largely that of a certain conflict of human temperaments: the 'tough-minded' and the 'tender minded.' Those with tough-minded approach to truth are often the empiricists who are committed to experience and often going by 'the facts.' They are more materialistic, pessimistic, irreligious, dogmatic, and fatalistic.

On the contrary, there are those with a tender-minded approach, who prefer *a priori* principles which appeal to reason and ratiocination. They also tend to be idealistic, optimistic, and religious, believing in free will.[220] In this situation therefore, what we have, is an empirical philosophy that is not religious enough and a religious philosophy that is not empirical enough. He believes there is a need to balance these extremes of approach to truth. This is because the two approaches have their values. The touch-minded adhere to facts while the tender-minded adhere to faith. There is need for a philosophy which adheres to facts and still finds room for faith, a philosophy capable of reconciling the "scientific loyalty to facts" with "the old confidence in human values." Such a mediating philosophy is seen in pragmatism where there is adherence to tough-minded epistemic standards that do not prevent the kind of worldview to which the tender-minded aspire. Pragmatism will accommodate the perspectives and values of any of the segments of approach for as long as they are useful in the

---

[220] Cf. Stumpf and Fieser, *Philosophy, History and Problems*, 377.

human practical life, as individuals or as community. For him, once we compare the practical consequences of both positions, we will find no conflict between them.

8.4 The Pragmatic Theory of Truth in Dewey (Instrumentalism)

John Dewey, though the last of the triumvirate of classical pragmatism, was the most influential, especially in the American school systems and political ideologies. He subscribes to the stance of Peirce that inquiry, whether scientific, technical, sociological, philosophical, or cultural is self-corrective over time. But this is, if openly submitted for testing by a community of inquirers to clarify, justify, refine, and/or refute proposed truth.[221] Dewey agrees with Peirce that truth is an outcome of scientific inquiry and consensus. Deweyan discussions on truth were mainly on his footnotes to the thoughts of Peirce and James on the theme. He technically used the term "Instrumentalism" to describe his own pragmatism.[222] His pragmatism strongly reflects the combination of Peirce and James. He tried to connect truth and rigorous scientific inquiry like Peirce while presenting the same truth as verified result of previous inquiry like James.

From the scientific inquiry, truth indicates not just an accepted belief, but a belief in virtue of a certain method. Truth shows a verified belief or proposition that comes from a certain procedure of inquiry and testing. Belief denotes the result of the best technique of inquiry available in some

---

[221] Cf. Encyclopedia of Philosophy, Vol.2, s.v. "Dewey, John."
[222] Cf. John Dewey, *The Quest for Certainty: A Study of the Relation of Knowledge and Action* (New York: GP Putnam's Sons, 1929). 3.

field. This implies that truth equates to scientific verification, where science emerges from and is continuous with everyday process of trial and error, leading to true propositions, which when acted on, can bring forth predictable and dependable outcomes. Scientific verification in Deweyan pragmatism means matching expectations with results. Truth is the "fate" of genuine scientific inquiry. It is the opinion which is fated to be ultimately agreed to by all who investigate, whereby the object represented by such an opinion is the real or reality. The term he often uses to describe this "fate" or end-in-view of scientific inquiry and consensus is "warranted assertibility."[223] Warranted assertibility as Dewey puts it is:

> Preferred to the terms *belief* and *knowledge* (because) it is free from the ambiguity of these latter terms, and it involves reference to inquiry as that which warrants assertion. When knowledge is taken as a general abstract term related to inquiry in the abstract, it means 'warranted assertibility.' The use of a term that designates potentiality rather than an actuality involves recognition that all special conclusions of special inquiries are parts of enterprise that is continually renewed or is a going concern.[224]

Dewey argues that the conventional philosophical terms such as "truth" and "knowledge" were filled with so many linguistic nuances that blur their practical roles which should be the emphasis. He smartly avoids speaking of *truth* when discussing the term. He preferred rather to focus on the functions played by truth in relation to meaning and human adaptation. Thus, his preference for the term,

---

[223] Cf. John Dewey, *Logic: The Theory of Inquiry* (New York: Henry Hold and Company, 1938), 9.
[224] Dewey, *Logic*, 9

"warranted assertibility" in capturing the meaning of true beliefs, which is the goal of scientific inquiry. Truth's function as the goal of inquiry is more important in the Deweyan pragmatic theory of truth than an ontological analysis of the concept of truth itself. He reserves the word "true" to the result of controlled inquiry like Peirce. Claims are only valid once verified, even though the verification process makes them trustworthy. It is why he also argues that only judgments, and not propositions, are the proper truth-bearers. For him, propositions are proposals and hypothesis used in the process of inquiry, which can then lead to conclusions and verified judgments, otherwise called truth. Propositions may be more or less relevant in inquiry but the truth or falsity of the process rests in the judgments or the settled outcome of inquiry (warranted assertibility).

Based on the above, Dewey holds that the pragmatic theory of truth is the one that merits properly to be called correspondence theory of truth because its conclusions are the products of the consensus or correspondence of different perspectives or dimensions of scientific inquiry. His idea of correspondence theory in this sense is the operational sense of the term, and not the empiricist or metaphysical notion of it. Correspondence of practical solutions from various scientific inquiries is the meaning of truth. True belief is not built on abstract statements but on sustained scientific investigation and examination pushed to its ultimate and indefeasible end. It is such that inquiry into truth must be controlled or directed to the transformation of an indeterminate situation into a determinate one, to convert elements of the original situation into a unified whole.

However, he is critical of the conventional correspondence theory of truth and the coherence theory of truth. He accuses the traditional correspondence theory of truth of being unnecessarily obscure, given that it depends so much on an abstract (often unverified) correspondence between a proposition and things out there. He equally criticizes empiricism, which mediates this theory, for being too fixed on experience for adaptability against other truth possibilities. On coherence theory and rationalism, which sustains it, he accuses them of presenting and confusing the meaning of knowledge when they define it without incorporating pragmatic possibilities.[225] As Stumpf and Fieser put it:

> He said, the empiricists assumed that thinking refers to fixed things in nature-that for each idea there is a corresponding something. It is as though knowing is modeled after what is supposed to happen when we look at something. Thus, to see something is to have an idea of it. This is called a 'spectator theory of knowledge.' But the rationalists argued that the reverse was true, namely, that when we have a clear idea, we are guaranteed that the object of our thought exists. In either case, empiricists, and rationalists both viewed the human mind as an instrument for considering what is fixed and certain in nature.[226]

For Dewey, the correspondence and coherence theories are static and mechanical and are mere *spectator theories or points of view* in verifying the truth. They do not touch on the real nature of things by way of being operational or helping humankind to cope with his or her environment. This is why he disqualified them as real bases of truth. On the contrary, he proposes that a better approach to truth is through *dynamic experience*.

---

[225] Cf. Stumpf and Fieser, *Philosophy, History and Problems*, 380.
[226] Stumpf and Fieser, *Philosophy, History and Problems*, 381.

Knowledge and Truth

Influenced by Darwinism, Dewey believes that human beings are like all other biological animals struggling for survival in their environment. The truth around humankind therefore must be derived from what helps him or her to survive in his or her existence. In this case, truth may not be limited to only one certainty but to as many things as useful in the survival of humankind. As Stumpf and Fieser observe: "Darwinian approach to knowledge influenced Dewey in the direction of pragmatism. Instead of pursuing a single ultimate truth about reality, his emphasis shifts to a pluralism of truths, many truths, and the characteristics that these ideas or notions are true because they 'work'."[227]

Dewey believes that there are several kinds of truth, even beyond the scientific method, if truth is whatever works for humankind in their struggle for survival and success. Discovering these survival instruments or kinds of truth is the business of science, while intelligently connecting them to experiences of humankind in life is the purpose of philosophy. Philosophical thinking must begin with our immediate, concrete life experiences.[228] And experience for him is what connects humankind as a dynamic biological entity with his precarious environment.[229] Experience provides us with the intelligence to cope with survival. And "human intelligence is the ability within us to cope with our environment. Thinking is not an individual act carried on in private or in isolation from practical problems. Instead, thinking, or active intelligence, arises in 'problem situations;' thinking

---

[227] Stumpf and Fieser, *Philosophy, History and Problems*, 454.
[228] Cf. Stumpf and Fieser, *Philosophy, History and Problems*, 454.
[229] Cf. Stumpf and Fieser, *Philosophy, History and Problems*, 381.

and doing are intimately related."[230] He divides thinking into two stages: the perplexed, troubled, and confused type at the beginning and the cleared-up, unified, resolved situation at the close.[231]

In his neologism of "instrumentalism" of pragmatism, he holds that "thinking is always instrumental in solving problems. Whereas empiricism and rationalism separate thinking and doing, instrumentalism holds that reflective thought is always involved in transforming a practical situation."[232] This is why thinking in Dewey's pragmatism is not a quest for truth, as though the truth were a static and eternal quality in things.[233] "Thinking, rather, is the act of trying to achieve an adjustment between individuals and their environment."[234] It is basically about changing conditions which requires changing judgments to maintain behavior that make for efficiency.[235] The central question therefore, in the Deweyan Instrumentalist concept of truth will be: "Does it end in conclusions which, when referred back to ordinary life-experiences and their predicaments, render them more significant, more luminous to us and make our dealings with them more fruitful?"[236] The Deweyan pragmatism or instrumentalism is a problem-solving theory of truth and knowledge. Truth is whatever helps one to survive and succeed through a precarious situation.

---

[230] Stumpf and Fieser, *Philosophy, History and Problems*, 381.
[231] Cf. Stumpf and Fieser, *Philosophy, History and Problems*, 381.
[232] Stumpf and Fieser, *Philosophy, History and Problems*, 381.
[233] Cf. Stumpf and Fieser, *Philosophy, History and Problems*, 381.
[234] Stumpf and Fieser, *Philosophy, History and Problems*, 381.
[235] Cf. Marc Tool, "John Dewey," in *Elgar Companion to Institutional and Evolutionary Economics* 1, ed. G.M. Hodgson (Northampton: Edward Elgar Publishing, 1994), 152ff.
[236] Stumpf and Fieser, *Philosophy, History and Problems*, 381.

In sum, Peirce, James, and Dewey are the greatest exponents that set the parameters for what makes a theory of truth pragmatic. There are some others too, but these three were the intellectual mainstays of the pragmatic theory of truth. Despite the significant differences in their respective accounts, their mainstream thought patterns on pragmatism remained remarkably similar. The first common thought is that they are all critical of traditional or conventional theories of truth: correspondence and coherence. They do not think that truth could be reduced to only agreement of thoughts to reality or consistency of thought with other thoughts. If these factors are present but do not have operational or functional implications for human practical life, then they are false or fictional.

They equally trusted in science as a method of truth, either as scientific community or individual inquiry, using scientific instruments. Pragmatism has strong faith in scientific truth, which is a product of intelligent consensus of experts and researchers. They equally agree that success and survival of the concrete person should be the focus of any true theory or proposition, and not really the judgment of a proposition as either true or false. Therefore, absolute certainties and entities of the transcendental realm may become true, when believing in them would lead to survival and success of humankind in their daily struggles. Metaphysical truths can be accepted by pragmatism where they help humankind to adapt and transform their lives and environment for a better situation. However, these points of pragmatism have attracted criticism.

8.5 Criticism of the Pragmatic Theory of Truth

Generally, pragmatic theory of truth has been criticized for paving way for relativism and pluralism of truth. As pointed by Eboh, pragmatism will lead to

> Relativism in that truth is defined in terms of utility, workability and successful results, there is the danger that there can be one truth for you and another for me. Such relativism will blind our judgements and make us less able to judge evidence impartially and objectively. But we ought to learn to view things as they are and control our hopes, wishes, cravings and prejudices.[237]

Relativism of truth based on usefulness can question and negate epistemic objectivity. Truth is an absolute notion. It will be absurd and, to some extent, a violation of the law of non-contradiction to say that something is "true for me but not for you" or that something is "true then and not now." Such relativism in truth will cancel one of the essential elements of truth, which is universality and perennial certainty.[238] And if truth is not universal and perennial, it means that it cannot be applied always to everyone and at all times. But this is not what the truth should be. Truth should be perennial, universal, consistent, certain, and general to every rational mind.[239] "Hence, utility, workability and satisfactory result cannot be the test of truth."[240] If truth is reduced to only what serves, it means that many things which are true in themselves will lose their epistemic and moral values. There are many religious, moral, and historical truths which may not have concrete

---

[237] Eboh, *Theory of Knowledge*, 47.
[238] Cf. Ani, *Introduction to Philosophy of History,* 167.
[239] Cf. Ani, *Introduction to Philosophy of history,* 167.
[240] Eboh, *Theory of Knowledge*, 47.

and practical values, but whose veracities are rationally justifiable.

Furthermore, the pragmatic theory of truth by Peirce has been criticized on the ground that he was not realistic enough. His stance that truth rests with the position where further inquiry becomes impossible is not tenable. How about certain truths which no one can inquire about or believe because the means and facts for their inquiries are either lost or not yet found? Handicap for further investigation cannot become a necessary justification for the acceptance of something as true or false. What we did not know centuries ago because there were no instruments of their investigation then, did not make the wrong claims of those centuries true because they could not have been investigated. The false stance that the earth was the center of the universe (*geocentrism*) eight centuries ago would not have been true then (just as it is still not true today) because there were no instruments of investigating the hypothesis then.

Even his claim on fallibilism is a weak reason to justify human limitation in pursuing the truth. His fallibilism argues that empirical knowledge can be accepted even though it cannot be proved with certainty. But will that also be a reason to decline the pursuance of certainty in other epistemic dimensions where the possibility and demand of certainty are expected or are possible? Intellective knowledge for instance, will require certainty for its veracity to be established, and it is possible to be achieved.

On James, one might accept that his idea of truth is psychologically satisfying but it is not realistic and fair enough on the epistemological concept of truth. Granted that true ideas may help us get things done, yet they may not tell us exactly what truth as an idea means. His pragmatic theory of truth fails to define and explain truth as truth. It only gave explanations on the uses or values of truth. He did not tell us what exactly constitutes truth or what makes an idea true. Furthermore, he seems to have equally reduced truth to collective name for verification processes. He holds that being verified is what makes an idea true. How about truths that are not verifiable as in self-evident truth or truths which are yet to have instruments for their verification? And though he criticizes the correspondence theory, his dedicated support for verification process and empirical concreteness in the qualification of truth argues for the same theory he sets out to criticize. This indicates some contradictions in his project and purpose. It is like criticizing and supporting the same theory.

Dewey has equally been criticized for equating truth with instruments that work. The fact remains that there are certain beliefs that are undeniably useful, but objectively they are false. One might accept the belief that it is the prayers that he or she says daily when he or she attends daily morning masses at a distant location that keep him or her fit. But the truth might be that it is the physical exercise associated with walking to the distant venue of the daily morning masses that keeps him or her fit. If he or she stops attending the daily morning masses at such a distant location, probably because the masses have been brought nearer to his or her residence, he or she might start getting fat and may have to rethink his or her earlier belief. A girl might find it helpful to believe that her prettiness is why so many suitors are after her, while in truth, her family's wealth could be the reason for the influx of many suitors for her. If something happens to the family's wealth, she might find out where the truth lies.

Having seen these critical points of the pragmatic theory of truth and the other classical theories of truth (correspondence and coherence), we can say that a more objective theory of truth must harness and incorporate the strengths in these theories of truth. Thus, truth must correspond with reality, cohere with reason and be appliable. It must agree with reality and be consistent with basic laws of reason and logic, while being relevant or existential to man. Eboh while searching for this more comprehensive notion of truth, explains that:

> Truth is the faithful adherence of our judgments and ideas to the facts or experience or to the world as it is: but since we cannot always compare our judgments with actual situations, we test them by consistency with other judgments that we believe are valid and true, or we test them by usefulness and practical experiences.[241]

In this explanation, one sees that the classical theories of truth do not really need to contradict each other. They can as well complement each other. They can mediate and enrich their positions and meanings. However, out of them, and somehow different from them too, there have been several other ancillary theories of truth, which are still focused on the epistemic project of clarifying and explaining the meaning of truth.

---

[241] Eboh, *Theory of Knowledge*, 49.

Chapter Nine: **Further Theories of Truth**

9.1 Supplementary Theories of Truth

Apart from the three principal theories of truth discussed already, there are other theories of truth in epistemology. These other ones are derived from the three main ones. They serve and support the principal propositions of the three main theories of truth, as either their subsidiary or supplementary theories. There are many of such supplementary theories in epistemology, but we shall limit our focus to the more conventional ones. Some of them which we shall briefly discuss include, the dialectical theory of truth, the pluralist theory of truth, the relativist theory of truth, the semantic theory of truth, the deflationist theory of truth and the consensus theory of truth.

9.2 Dialectical Theory of Truth

The dialectical theory of truth views truth as correspondence of knowledge to objective reality as seen in the process of becoming since reality itself is becoming. This is partly rooted in correspondence theory of truth. It also sees truth as a product of dialectics, logically, idealistically, or existentially. Elements of it can be seen in Plato's dialectics where a process of logical dialogues can generate truth. In Hegelian dialectical idealism, one also sees this theory of truth in the dialectics of the Spirit which is constantly evolving and developing itself through the dialectical process.²⁴² According to Hegel, knowing the dialectics and dynamics of the development of the Spirit which is the totality of reality is what truth is all about.²⁴³ In a related manner, Karl Marx's dialectical materialism equally exemplifies the dialectical theory of truth. Truth for Marx is the understanding of the dialectical process of the material forces, and how they help in the economic emancipation of man through labor.²⁴⁴

9.3 Pluralist Theory of Truth

The pluralist theory of truth holds that there may be more than one means or category that makes a proposition true. It argues that there is no one key to the truth – truth is an epistemic function that may be demonstrated in several ways. For every expression of truth, there is a different definition of the criteria, adapted to the different discussion topics. Truth therefore is multivalent and as such, there are multiple means of truth. This multiplicity concept of truth is the reason for the wide range diversity of truth in line with specific truth of a discourse or discipline. This is why one can talk about truth in relation to a particular field of human existentiality, like talking about moral truth, religious truth, judicial truth, cultural truth, artistic truth, political truth, scientific truth, philosophical truth, theological truth, national security truth etc. Pluralist theory of truth simply subscribes to the logic that there are variety of ways that can be used to determine the value of truth. Such ways may be

---

[242] Cf. Humphrey Uchenna Ani, *Discourses on Philosophy of History, A Study of Critical Conceptualizations on History* (Enugu: PUKKA Press, 2021), 14.
[243] Cf. Omoregbe, *Epistemology*, 44.
[244] Cf. Ani, *Discourses on Philosophy of History*, 67ff.

rational, factual, coherent, pragmatic, moral, social, etc. Sometimes these criteria or ways may complement each other. Rational criteria for instance can complement moral ones in defining the truth.

The Pluralist theory of truth essentially denies the general assumption often found among the main or classical theories of truth that one factor or property can justify the truth. The coherence theory argues that only coherence to a set of true propositions makes a proposition true. The correspondence theory argues that it is only conformity of proposition to objective reality that makes it true. The pragmatic theory holds that it is only practical utility that makes proposition true etc. They all represent a kind of monistic argument that there is one and only one factor that is sufficient to provide the property of truth in a statement. Contrary to them, the pluralist theory argues that propositions might be true due to more than one category. It maintains that more than one factor can combine in the making of a true proposition. A statement can be true by being coherent, by corresponding to a fact or data, and by being useful, all together. It affirms that the making of a true proposition requires more than one property.

In his 1992 work, *Truth and Objectivity*, Crispin Wright strongly argues for, and supported this pluralism of the conditions of truth. He argues that any predicate that satisfies certain platitudes about truth should be counted as truth predicate and be made part of the conditions for affirming or justifying the truth of a proposition. He used the term "superassertibility" to qualify the role of truth predicate in a proposition.[245] A truth predicate becomes

---

[245] Cf. Crispin Wright, *Truth and Objectivity*. Cambridge: Harvard University Press, 1992), 3.

superassertible when it does not change the truth value of a statement, even when the statement has become enlarged and improved upon. In that case there are many truth predicates which are superassertible and combine in one statement to justify its truth. Michael Lynch in his *Truth as One and Many* equally argues that truth is a functional property capable of being multiply manifested in distinct and different properties, which could be pragmatic, coherence, correspondence etc.[246]

9.4 Relativist Theory of Truth

There is also the relativist theory of truth as propounded by the Ghanaian philosopher, Kwasi Wiredu in his 1980 work, *Philosophy, and an African Culture*. He posits in this work that there is no difference between truth and opinion.[247] According to him, whatever is referred to as truth is more correctly interpreted as opinion or point of view, given that history has shown that what human beings consider to be true can be argued to be false from another point of view. By this assertion that truth is equivalent to opinion, Wiredu *ipso facto*, rejects the "objectivist theory" of truth, which he describes as holding that "once a proposition is true, it is true in itself and forever. Truth, in other words, is timeless, eternal."[248] An objectivist theory of truth would imply that truth is categorically distinct from opinion.[249] The objectivist theory is contrary to Wiredu's relativism of truth which argues that truth arises from

---

[246] Cf. Michael Lynch, *Truth as One and Many*. Oxford: Oxford University Press, 2009),4.
[247] Cf. Kwasi Wiredu, *Philosophy and an African Culture* (Cambridge: Cambridge University Press, 1980), 124.
[248] Wiredu, *Philosophy and an African Culture*, 114.
[249] Cf. Wiredu, *Philosophy and an African Culture*, 115.

human agency that is different, unique, relative, and not from transcendental reality. Thus, whatever is called truth is someone's truth. Therefore, "we must recognize the cognitive element of point of view as intrinsic to the concept of truth."[250] The implication is that truth is relative and subjective. It is tantamount to opinion. And as he said "What I mean by opinion is a firm rather than an uncertain thought. I mean what is called a considered opinion."[251] In his theory of truth, "There are as many truths as there are points of view."[252] As Omoregbe presents it:

> Wiredu rejects what he calls the objectivist view of truth, which sees truth as an independent, objective reality, timeless, eternal, and unchanging. The objectivist view makes a categorical distinction between truth and opinion. 'But if truth is categorically different from opinion,' Wiredu continued, then 'truth is, as a matter of logical principle, unknowable... If anybody claims to know the truth about anything, he is simply putting forward his opinion as truth. Any given claim to truth is merely an opinion advanced from specific point of view.'[253]

9.5 Semantic Theory of Truth

There is the semantic theory of truth (linguistic theory of truth). It is mainly credited to the Polish American mathematician, logician and philosopher, Alfred Tarski (1901-1983) who propounded this theory while investigating problems associated with the definability of real numbers. He concluded that finding the definition of

---

[250] Wiredu, *Philosophy and an African Culture*, 115.
[251] Wiredu, *Philosophy and an African Culture*, 115-116.
[252] Wiredu, *Philosophy and an African Culture*, 115.
[253] Omoregbe, *Epistemology*, 46-47.

real numbers can help in the definition of truth also. In this process, he wanted to find out what it means to understand and define truth. Initially, he tried using the concepts of correspondence theory, but later dropped the idea, maintaining the use of semantic analysis of implications of propositions and their true values. But in fact, his theory actually took a lot from the correspondence theory, which is why many scholars believe that his theory is a version of correspondence theory.[254] Some argue that the difference between the two theories rests on the point that while the correspondence theory depends on physical fact for its veracity with a statement, the semantic theory depends on the sentential assertion or function of the metalanguage of a statement to be true.

Semantic theory defines the criteria that will be met for something to be true. It identifies truth to be contained in sentences (semantic structures), especially the metalinguistic part of a sentence. This implies that truth is not contained in judgements but in the structures of sentences. If I say for instance that "Boston College is in Massachusetts" and I want to evaluate the conditions under which it can be true, this theory will argue that the statement, "Boston College is in Massachusetts" is true, if and only if Boston College is in Massachusetts. In this statement, according to Tarski, there are two orders of speaking (predication). There is the first order sentence (ordinary language sentence), "Boston College is in Massachusetts." And there is the second order sentence (metalinguistic sentence), "Boston College is in Massachusetts, if and only if it is true that Boston College

---

[254] Cf. Alfred Tarski, "The Semantic Conception of Truth," in *Philosophy and Philosophical Research*, 4 (1944): 342.

is in Massachusetts." This statement can be expressed in this form:

1. The sentence "Boston College is in Massachusetts" is true.
2. If and only if,
3. It is true that "Boston College is in Massachusetts."

In this form, **line 1** is about the truth, **line 2** is about the conditions for the truth, and **line 3** is about asserting a fact in Massachusetts (which is true). What this means is that the truth of the proposition rests in the assertion contained in the metalinguistic sentence in **line 3**, which confirms what is judged to be true in **line 1**.

Thus, "the theory makes truth a property of sentences rather than [what is] found in judgements. The theory implies that to say that something is true is to make an assertion about a sentence."[255] Truth, therefore, is a metalinguistic adjective qualifying a judgement or claim. This semantic truth theory reveals that it is the logic of the sentential structure within propositions that makes valid reasoning to preserve truth.

Tarski equally tries to use the theory to resolve the problem of "paradox of a liar," by distinguishing what is said in ordinary language and what is said in meta-language (metalinguistic) sentences. A classic example of this was the famous paradox of Epimenides, a Cretan who said that all Cretans are liars. "He, being a Cretan, is also a liar, which means that his statement is a lie because it is true that all

---

[255] Omoregbe, *Epistemology*, 45.

Cretans are liars."[256] His theory of truth had also influenced other epistemologists in this regard like Saul Kripke.

9.6 Deflationary or Minimalist Theory of Truth

There is also the deflationary theory of truth. It was mainly propagated by linguistic epistemologists like Gottlob Frege, Frank P. Ramsey, and Paul Horwich. The stance of this theory of truth is that assertions of truth predicate like "it is true," "it is evident," or "it is false" and similar prefixes for truth or falsity to statements do not add or contribute to the attribute of truth in such statements. To assert that a statement is true is just to assert the statement itself. If I say that *it is true* that I am from Egede in Enugu, it is equivalent to saying simply that I am from Egede in Enugu. The prefix "it is true…" is unnecessary or uncalled for according to this theory. It is redundant in defining or asserting the veracity of where I come from, which is Egede in Enugu. This is why this theory is also called *the redundancy theory of truth*, especially the version championed by Frank P. Ramsey.

The theory also denies that truth has any underlying nature, therefore, truth predicate exists solely for certain logical needs like making explicit formulation of schematic generalizations of statements. Truth predicates are only for logical explications and distinctions, and as such do not add or contribute to the truth value of statements. According to this theory, "It is true that Bigard is a seminary means no more than that Bigard is a seminary," and "It is false that Bigard is a seminary simply means that Bigard is not a seminary," and nothing more. The truth predicates (it is

---

[256] Omoregbe, *Epistemology*, 45.

true... and it is false...) do not add anything new to the statement, rather they are redundant and minimal to the alethic formula in the statements. Statements will be true even in the most minimal sentences without the truth predicates like "it is true," it is false," "it is evident" etc. Hence, it is also called the *minimalist theory of truth*. This brand of deflationary theory was championed by Paul Horwich. He argues for instance that truth predicate is indeed a property of propositions, but it is so minimal and anomalous a predicate that it cannot be said to provide one with any new alethic or useful insight or information about the proposition. Other names of the deflationary theory of truth include: the *disappearance theory*, *the no-truth theory* and *the disquotational theory*.

Irrespective of whatever names or versions they may be, the central argument of the deflationary theory of truth is that truth has no other nature beyond what is captured in ordinary statements like saying "I am from Egede in Enugu." I need no further truth predicate or criteria to validate that it is true. This is why the deflationists are against the various theories of truth that call for extra proofs or criteria (the inflationary theories) like the correspondence, the coherence, and the pragmatic theories. According to deflationary theory, truth does not consist in correspondence to the facts (correspondence theory). It does not consist in coherence with a set of beliefs or propositions (coherence theory). It does not consist of practical usefulness (pragmatic theory). These suggestions are mistaken according to the Deflationists because they assume that truth has a nature that does need those theories to define it. For the Deflationists, truth has no special nature. Truth is simply captured, founded, and expressed in ordinary language.

Some versions of deflationary theory include the redundancy type, the performative type, and the pro-sentential type. For the redundancy type, if I say that 4+4 =8, then 4+4=8. It is redundant to add the truth prefix "*it is true* that 4+4=8." The performative type was advocated for by Peter Strawson. His main argument is that ascribing truth predicate to a proposition is not really characterizing the proposition itself, nor is it saying something redundant. It is rather saying something about the intention of the speaker. [257] The truth predicates in statements have performatory function whereby they add some function to their sentences like concession, agreement, or denial. If I say, "I agree," "it is true," "I concede" before a sentence, it adds something of my intention and responsibility or performance to the sentence. The truth predicates or prefixes in this case endorse the intention of the speaker in the sentences. There is a whole lot of difference when I say, "I will give you money" and when I say, "I agree that I will give you money." The other version is the pro-sentential type that argues that all uses of "it is true" in sentences are pro-sentential and they invite the attention of the listener to the person of the speaker. They represent the speaker like in pronoun.

9.7 Consensus Theory of Truth

The consensus theory of truth holds that truth depends on what everyone agrees to be true. It is an ancient theory of truth termed in Latin as *consensus gentium*, (agreement of the people). Its main argument is that whatever is universal or general among people carries the weight of truth. Consensus theory of truth may have varied basis

---

[257] Cf. Omoregbe, *Epistemology*, 46.

depending on its peculiar criterion. In some cases, the criterion of universal consent is taken strictly, while in others, it might be softer. What may determine the nature of consensus could be the specific population deciding over a given question, the proportion of the population required for consensus to be reached, or the period needed to declare a consensus. Instances of the consensus theory of truth are seen in various aspects of our daily lives. Many people believe that eating less or no sugar will be good for their bodies because experts in medicine and nutrition have subscribed to that. They may not have experimented on this or even done their personal diagnosis, to really know what their bodies really need. They may just accept the proposition or stance as true because it is the consensus of experts, and based on that, they may stop eating sugar.[258]

Most things people accept to be true on an expertise basis are sustained by the consensus theory of truth, not really on correspondence or coherence grounds. Some may not have been verified or been experimented on, for reliability and correctness. Consensus of scientists and experts, assisted by research, often shape the nature of truth or knowledge people believe in. We believe in the information of astronomers on the nature and shape of the universe, even though we may not have been in outer space to verify what we are told about them. We accept such things to be true simply because people agree upon them. Consensus theory could be actual or ideal. An actual consensus is based on actual human development, while an ideal consensus could be based on such intellectual

---

[258] Cf. Cedric Chin, Thinking Better, *The Four Theories of Truth as a Method for Critical Thinking* https://commoncog.com/four-theories-of-truth/

operations as abstraction, extrapolation, and idealization of actual conditions of situation or society.

One of the major criticisms of consensus theory of truth is that it does not often define how we know that a consensus is achieved. In some cases, consensus may not have justification in correspondence to any reality or coherence to any principle. It can be in error because it is not often discovered through scientific experiments and observation or an already existing principle. Its pure empirical form might mean that a statement can be true even if it fails to describe any reality. The theory may sometimes run counter to even self-evident truth, especially where force or mass mobilization is used to attain consensus truth as seen in most social issues. Imre Lakatos describes this theory as a "watered down" form of provable truth enabled and shared by social epistemologists like Thomas Kuhn and Michael Polanyi."[259] Nigel Warburton argues that the theory is not reliable because people are often prone to a dream and can believe any assertion and espouse it as truth in the face of overwhelming evidence and facts to the contrary. People are also prone to gullibility and can easily be misled by general opinion not founded on reliable facts and evidence.[260]

The scientific community criteria of truth propounded by Charles Sanders Pierce in pragmatism is a typical example of consensus theory of truth. He may not have used the term in describing his theory of truth or pragmatism, but the idea in his stance subscribes strongly to

---

[259] Imre Lakatos, "Falsification and the Methodology of Scientific Research Programme," in *Philosophical Papers* (Cambridge: Cambridge University Press,1978), 8.
[260] Cf. Nigel Warburton, "Truth by Consensus," in *Thinking from A to Z* (London: Routledge,2000), 134-135.

consensus theory. He argues that truth depends on the corporate or collective conclusion after a scientific investigation of a matter. For him, it is the conclusion of the community of inquiry that determines what is true. He writes that "conclusions of science, then, must be conclusions that all scientists can draw. Similarly, in questions of belief and truth, it should be possible for anyone to come to the same conclusions."[261] Truth becomes justified when everyone can arrive at it from different fields of investigation or inquiry, especially where they have carried out their empirical investigation on the matter to arrive at their conclusion. For him, a statement is true if and only if it is agreed to by all those who investigate it. Jurgen Habermas also advocates for this theory when he argues that truth must be agreed to by all investigators who adopted the principle of equal, unconstrained, undistorted, and discursive method in their inquiry before a conclusion.

However, the principal and ancillary theories of truth, especially in the conventional, often western scholarship, do not exhaust the search for truth through epistemology. There have also been other fields of study of human knowledge which may not have been captured within the curriculum of conventional studies, especially in the western or global North epistemologies. In fact, the western canon of scholarship is often accused of exercising epistemicide, which refers to the deliberate silencing, violation, suppression, and destruction of knowledge system of other civilizations. Western and mainstream epistemology have often been accused of monopolization and colonization of epistemological methods and merit, leaving the less popular ones in eclipse. Thus, prompting a

---

[261] Stumpf and Fieser, *Philosophy, History and Problems*, 374.

decolonization of epistemology has become a new movement in the course. There are many forgotten and neglected epistemological systems, especially among indigenous communities round the world which are receiving serious attention and interest in epistemology.

Epistemology today, therefore, is expanding its frontiers of academic inquiry to the study of indigenous knowledge systems in many societies of the world. It is in such new systems of epistemology that one might locate some current studies on African epistemology. And related to that are emerging issues in epistemology emanating from new digital technology and new world order cultures like artificial intelligence and post-truth phenomenon. The issues and debates in these non-conventional fields of epistemic studies constitute part of the problems or challenges in examining human knowledge and formulating formulae of truth in epistemology today. They are at the heart of the problems of human knowledge in contemporary epistemology in philosophy.

PART THREE: ALTERNATIVES TO TRADITIONAL EPISTEMOLOGY

Chapter Ten: **Indigenous knowledge Systems and** *Akonuche*

10.1 Epistemicide

The background of studies in non-conventional themes or alternative topics in epistemology like the *Indigenous Knowledge Systems* is motivated by new developments in global evolution of the human society. Traditional epistemology has been dominated by Western methods and scholarship of the global North. It has also thrived on the disparagement of the other systems of epistemology in some other axis of the globe. For centuries, epistemological methods and conceptualizations peculiar to Indigenous societies have been submerged under pernicious process of epistemic denigration and in some cases, outright, denial. Recently, however, there is high awareness of the age long trend in the history of epistemology, of the deliberate attempt, especially by occidental scholars to downgrade or even destroy knowledge systems that may not have met the conventional criteria, often associated with classical Western thoughts. This has created a negative development which in contemporary epistemology is identified as epistemicide. What is it all about? How is it executed? How is it identified in the current study of human knowledge, and what are the implications it has in contemporary studies on the problem of human knowledge? How did it spur studies on Indigenous Knowledge Systems? And how did it motivate studies in alternative epistemologies?

Epistemicide is derived from two Greek terms: *episteme* (belief or knowledge) and – *caedere* (to kill) or *cide* (killing) which has to do with killing, like one talking about homicide, infanticide, insecticide etc. As a term in epistemology, epistemicide was coined and propagated by the Portuguese sociologist Boaventura de Sousa Santos.[262] By this coinage, he refers to the destruction of existing knowledge system by some means and for some reasons. He applied the word in the context of colonisation which he argues has brought violence against other forms of human knowledge in many parts of the globe, especially against the Indigenous knowledge systems of the people of the global South. In his book, *Epistemologies of the South: Justice Against Epistemicide,* he argues that the dispossession of other knowledge system leads to killing of their knowledge system which he describes as epistemicide.[263] He explores the concept of 'cognitive injustice' which is embedded in the failure to recognize the different ways of knowing and making meaning of their world by different kinds of people across the world.

Sousa Santos argues that global social justice can only be possible when there is global cognitive justice. He observes that the profound knowledge system in the global South has been dominated and marginalized by Western epistemology. He posits that it has become imperative in our contemporary society to recover and value the epistemological plurality across the world. Unlike the epistemology of the West that is rational, logical, market

---

[262] Cf. Boaventura de Sousa Santos, *Epistemologies of the South, Justice Against Epistemicide,* ed. Maria Paula Meneses (New York: Routledge, 2014), 1.
[263] Cf. B.L. Hall, and R. Tandon, "Decolonization of Knowledge, Epistemicide, Participatory Research and Higher Education," in *Research for All*, 1 (1), (2017): 8.

driven and individualistic, he notes that the epistemology of the South is cosmopolitan, communal, democratic, and as such enhances epistemic conviviality, solidarity, and life value.

Epistemicide involves destroying, marginalizing, banishing alternative or indigenous, subaltern, and counter-hegemonic forms of knowledge. This knowledge destruction is perpetuated through epistemic injustices, which are the ways we harm knowers in the process of their epistemological development. Epistemic injustices, of course, can influence the prioritization and politicization of epistemic faculties and possibilities, thereby shaping our shared understandings of human intellectual and cultural heritage. When the global North colonized the global South, they did not just appropriate their natural resources. They changed their ecological and epistemological horizons to maximize their interests, thus, leading to epistemicide, or the killing of Indigenous knowledge systems in the global South. The denigration of Indigenous knowledge systems and the colonization of the natives for instance led to the abandonment of their native agro-ecology techniques and values. This is the case of the Milpa in Mexico, Waru Waru in Peru, and Zai or Tassa (*knowledge* on restoring degraded dryland and to increase fertility) in Western Sahel countries like Niger and Mali.[264]

Sousa Santos holds that Western epistemicide deliberately kills, silences, annihilates and devalues the knowledge system that does not match its yardstick. Sometimes it may relegate other forms of knowledge

---

[264] Cf. "Sourcebook of Alternative Technologies for Freshwater Augmentation in Africa," United Nations Environment Programme. Archived from the original on 26 March 2003. Retrieved 11 December 2016.

outside its standards to witchcraft, tradition, superstition, folkways, and mere common sense. Eurocentric epistemology is as real as colonial political practices created by the Eighteenth and Nineteenth centuries domination of global economy by the Western nations. Political colonization, no doubt, creates colonization of intellectual energy and knowledge possibility. The danger of this epistemological murder and devaluation of indigenous knowledge is that the natives are made to feel that they are not authorities in their own experiences and expertise. Thus, the knowledge they can contribute to the global epistemic system is destroyed and lost to humankind. Epistemicide suppresses the epistemic agency of the minority people, while elevating that of the powerful ones. Of course, it occurs because there is epistemic injustice and epistemic violence.

In epistemic injustice, there is harm done to impede recognizing a people's capacity to know or exercise knowledge of their own in their world. It is the "wrong done to someone specifically in his or her capacity as a knower."[265] Epistemic injustice can come in different forms. Miranda Fricker observes two forms of epistemic injustice, which include: testimonial injustice and hermeneutical injustice.[266] *Testimonial injustice* occurs when "prejudice" causes the receiver of the information "to give a deflated

---

[265] Cf. Beth Patin, Melinda Sebastian, Jieun Yeon, Danielle Bertolini and Alexandra Grimm, "Interrupting Epistemicide: A Practical Framework for Naming, Identifying, and Ending Epistemic Injustice in the Information Professions," in SURFACE at Syracuse University School of Information Studies - Faculty Scholarship, 2.

[266] Cf. Miranda Fricker, (1999), Epistemic Oppression and Epistemic Privilege," *Canadian Journal of Philosophy*, 29 (suppl 1), 191–210. https:// doi.org/10.1080/00455091.1999.10716836

level of credibility to a speaker's world."²⁶⁷ *Hermeneutical injustice* happens, "when a gap in collective interpretative resources puts someone at an unfair disadvantage when it comes to making sense of their social experiences."²⁶⁸ There is also the *curricular injustice* when physical resources are not available to help support epistemic growth. And finally, there is *participatory injustice* such as the exclusion of one's participation in their own epistemological development.²⁶⁹

In epistemic violence, there is the deliberate denial of a people, a voice to speak for themselves on issues concerning what they know. The term, "epistemic violence" became popularized from the postcolonial Theorist Gayatri Chakravorty Spivak in her famous essay "Can the Subaltern Speak."²⁷⁰ She tries to identify the "subaltern" who is the marginalized with no voice over his affairs. This silencing of the subaltern class is tantamount to epistemic violence, whereby they are removed from their ability to speak for themselves on every level. This involves destroying their systems of knowledge, beliefs, traditions, and language.

The Black feminist philosopher, Kristie Dotson also posits that epistemic violence is a form of pernicious ignorance that occurs when dominant hearers refuse to meet marginalized speakers "halfway" or on their own or some compromised epistemic turf between them. She calls it a kind of "reliable ignorance," that is, ignorance you can expect to be present—or used, but which does harm through

---

[267] Patin et al, "Interrupting Epistemicide, 3.
[268] Patin et al, "Interrupting Epistemicide, 3.
[269] Cf. Patin et al, "Interrupting Epistemicide, 3.
[270] Gayatri Chakravorty Spivak, "Can the Subaltern Speak?" ed. Amber Husain and Mark Lewis, *Two Works Series Volume One* (Koln: Afterall Books, 2021),1ff.

the alleged power dynamics between groups in the situation. It is a kind of violence being done to the allegedly unheard members of oppressed society. Dotson claims that dominant groups reliably and maliciously ignore the testimony of members of marginalized groups. Thus, in the wake of the dangers of epistemicide and its concomitant effects of epistemic injustice, epistemic violence and epistemic colonization, some scholars have risen to challenge different epistemological forms of oppression, by producing the idea of decolonization of epistemology. The idea is to free epistemology from a monolithic western tradition, and to inject alternative methods and modes in the study of human knowledge as seen in other spheres of the globe.

10.2 Epistemological Decolonization

The main mission of studies in Indigenous Knowledge Systems is to decolonize epistemology from occidental monolithic scholarship. Epistemic or epistemological decolonization is a recent term in epistemology advanced in decolonial scholarship that critiques epistemicide and the perceived hegemony and control of global knowledge system by occidental epistemology. It is about the interrogation of the accustomed categories and concepts of comprehension and reflection. How do we think in a way different from the conventional-often western versions? This process means making a change in basic assumptions in the way in which knowledge is thought and constructed. And it aims at incorporating a wider horizon from different axes of the globe. It implies a change of horizon from the traditional forms and formulations of epistemological methods and measures.

Epistemological decolonization has to do with a cancellation of the subalternation of minority or Indigenous knowledge system, so that all epistemic formulae can be represented in their strengths and lapses. To decolonize epistemology would require de-racialization, de-masculinization, and de-westernization of epistemic structures of conceptualization and communication, so that human knowledge can have a truly universal face. It demands expanding the horizon of epistemology so that the hegemonic theories, ontologies, methodologies, systems, objects, themes, and questions that are the study of human knowledge can welcome new and inclusive means and systems. Epistemology would be more dynamic if it welcomes differences and diversities. Working for an epistemology in which knowledge is studied from the intelligent minds of the academia and the local community's thinkers is one of the possible goals of epistemic decolonization. Experiments on these are what inspired the recovery and sustained studies in Indigenous Knowledge Systems, which is a topical theme in contemporary epistemology. What does this alternative version of epistemology mean? What are its implications? What constitutes the nature and purpose of studies in Indigenous Knowledge Systems?

10.3 Indigenous Knowledge Systems

Indigenous knowledge systems (IKS) simply refer to an epistemology that studies the indigenous knowledge unique to a particular locality, culture, or society. This new dimension of epistemology is recent and is inspired by the presumption that there exist other epistemologies or ways of representing knowledge outside the conventional and classical means as seen often in western scholarship. It is an epistemological step in the process of decolonization of the knowledge system in a transformative way. As B.L. Hall and R. Tandon note, it is encouraged through more profound attention to knowledge democracy and public engagement in knowledge sharing, which discourages epistemicide and raises more profound questions on the relations of knowledge to power.[271] United Nations Educational, Scientific, and Cultural Organization (UNESCO) on IKS says:

> Local and indigenous knowledge refers to the understandings, skills and philosophies developed by societies with long histories of interaction with their natural surroundings. For rural and indigenous peoples, local knowledge informs decision-making about fundamental aspects of day-to-day life.[272]

It is a kind of knowledge which is integral to a cultural complex. It encompasses language, systems of classification, resource use practices, social interactions, ritual, and spirituality. These unique methods of knowing are significant dimensions of the world's cultural diversity, and they provide a foundation for locally appropriate sustainable development.[273] Helen Thomas explains that,

> Indigenous Knowledge Systems is a phrase that originated in Indigenous studies. I could describe it to you using academic terms such as epistemology, ontology, and axiology. But Indigenous Knowledge Systems are the ways that Indigenous peoples make sense

---

[271] Cf. Hall, and Tandon, "Decolonization of Knowledge," 7.
[272] "Local and Indigenous Knowledge Systems (LINKS)," in UNESCO, Indigenous People's International Decade of Indigenous Languages (IDIL, 2022/2032) //en.unesco.org/links, accessed 3 March 2024.
[273] Cf. United Nations Educational, Scientific, and Cultural Organization Definitions of Traditional Knowledge.

of the world around them, and how they recognize, value, share and use knowledge in their daily lives. The phrase is intentionally plural to honor the diversity of Indigenous nations.[274]

It is generally a place-based kind of knowledge. It is often based on oral traditions and kinship and reflects on the unique experiences of each indigenous community, while sharing common traits of cognitive definition. Its method of inquiry could be by participatory research from the members of the community, which makes its knowledge generation co-productive and democratic in approach. Thus, it operates with a kind of knowledge democracy whereby there is an acknowledgment of the importance of multiple knowledge systems, such as organic, spiritual, and land-based frameworks arising from social movements and experiences. It has unrestricted access for the sharing of knowledge, making it a powerful tool for acting in social movements to deepen epistemic democracy for a fairer and healthier community.[275]

IKS has some essential characteristics. It is historically rooted in the sense that it derives its sources from historical experiences of the indigenous community, and how those historical experiences help them to adapt to their social, political, economic, environmental, moral, and spiritual changes. It is a type of knowledge that helps a community to survive and master their immediate environment. It is also cumulative and traditional because its epistemic structures and skills are products of centuries

---

[274] Helen Thomas, "Indigenous Knowledge Is Often Overlooked in Education. But It Has a Lot to Teach Us," in *Edsurge*, https://www.edsurge.com/news/2022-01-13-indigenous-knowledge-is-often-overlooked-in-education-but-it-has-a-lot-to-teach-us.
[275] Cf. Hall and Tandon, "Decolonization of Knowledge," 6.

of cumulative experiments and learning from immediate nature and society. This cumulative adaptiveness makes IKS very dynamic because it evolves, adapts, and grows across ages as society grows too. It is not a static form of knowledge. This is part of why it is intergenerational in nature, as it passes on the collective memory within a given community, from one generation to the next. It can do this by oral tradition of stories, songs, ceremonies, rituals, folktales, legends, and proverbs.

IKS is very empirical, and experiential given that its inquiries and intelligence is derived from empirical observation. Indigenous knowledge seekers engage in observing their environment and society, and from such observations, they draw their conclusions and make their decisions for their society. However, this mode of inquiry and thrust of veracity are relative to the various ages in the society in most IKS. This is why the elderly generation are often more relied upon in the possession of knowledge than the younger ones.

Most forms of IKS are not differentiated in mode. They are often holistic because they connect every axis of the people's life. Objects of understanding are not treated or perceived in isolation as often seen in classical empiricism or rationalism. Objects of knowing are taken as whole, and as parts of bigger whole of the community. The world is seen in its integral whole. This is why IKS incorporates empirical, rational, historical, cultural, social, and spiritual dimensions in its effort to understand the object of inquiry. Thus, making its intentionality cyclic across all the structures of society. Its intentionality is not linear in form. It carries all elements of nature and society together while searching for a holistic comprehension of questions and issues that challenge society. This is very sustainable in relation to natural, social, and economic activities of humankind. This is why its cognitional faculties are also governed by moral demands.

IKS mediates between epistemology and ethics in its reason and action, demanding responsibility for its epistemic conclusions. However, every form of IKS is unique to the culture and community where it is born and expressed, depending on the lived experiences of each community that generated the knowledge. There could be IKS of native Americans, IKS of Aborigine Australians, IKS of Latin Americans, IKS of Indians/Asians, IKS of Africans, and IKS of Europeans (especially those whose native knowledge systems have not featured in the classical traditions of philosophy). Besides studies in IKS, studies in African epistemology are another significant alternative forms of epistemology in contemporary philosophy.

10.4 African Epistemology

African epistemology, though profound and critical in its traditions and history, has also been subjugated by western dominated scholarship in conventional epistemology for centuries. Renewed awareness and the need to revive the suppressed axis of human studies have brought new engagements with African epistemology. This has been enabled mainly by decolonial studies on African scholarship and the global South in general. African epistemology is derived from and rooted in African philosophy and ontology. It is the body of epistemological experiences, beliefs, and attitudes of the African embedded in his philosophy. As Paul O. Irikefe explains, African epistemology has to do with the

Study of phenomenon of knowledge from an African perspective, where this is to be understood as the perspective of the individual African philosopher rooted in a historical and cultural consciousness, or those of various African communities, or experts in those communities. In the contemporary era, African epistemology involves three distinct, but interrelated projects: ethno-epistemology, analytic African epistemology, and ameliorative African epistemology.[276]

He further explains that *ethno-epistemology* deals with the study of knowledge from the perspective of particular African communities as revealed in their cultural heritage, proverbs, folklores, traditions, and practices as seen in Placide Tempel's *Bantu* Philosophy. Then, the *analytic African epistemology* involves the philosophical study of epistemic concepts, such as "knowledge," "justification," "belief" and "truth" from the African perspective, using the methods of analysis, criticism, arguments, ordinary language philosophy, and so on.[277] Here one might find the ideas of African epistemologists like Hallen and Sodipo's *Yoruba Epistemology* and Amechi Udefi's *Igbo Epistemology*.[278] The third dimension is what he termed *ameliorative African epistemology*, which in his thinking explores the predicament of African knowledge systems and voices in the global knowledge economy. It does this within the broader context of the problem of epistemic injustice suffered by historically marginalized groups.[279] The African epistemologies done in this regard

---

[276] Paul O. Irikefe, "African Epistemology," (Forthcoming in) *The Blackwell Companion to Epistemology, 3rd Edition*, ed. Kurt Sylvan, Matthias Steup, Ernest Sosa, and Jonathan Dancy, 1.
[277] Cf. Irikefe, African Epistemology, 6.
[278] Cf. Irikefe, *African Epistemology*, 6.
[279] Cf. Irikefe, *African Epistemology*, 8.

may include the works of some Africans in diaspora and the wider scope of studies of marginalized scholarship of the global South as depicted in such writers as Boaventura de Sousa Santos (2013, 2018), Ramón Grosfoguel (2007, 2013), Anibal Quijano (2000), and Walter Mignolo (2002, 2009).[280]

African epistemology, similar to, but different from the IKS is holistic and traditional. Its holistic nature is derived from its holistic ontology, given that every epistemology is often rooted in its metaphysics which constitutes and provides the object of its epistemic intentionality. The African ontology which provides the epistemic content and objects of knowing is not only holistic, but hierarchical, flowing from a descending order of God, divinities, ancestors, humans, animals, plants and minerals.[281] This hierarchy as Emmanuel Etta and Asukwo Offiong observe is such that "the superior forces have a direct influence on the lower ones which can only influence the higher forces indirectly through spiritual works or otherwise."[282]

Embedded in an African holistic ontology, African epistemology studies human knowledge as an aspect of the ontological oneness of being. Thus, Bert Hamminga remarks on African epistemology that, "knowledge is one form of togetherness. Togetherness is our ultimate criterion of any action, the pursuit of knowledge being just one of

---

[280] Cf. Irikefe, *African Epistemology*, 8.
[281] Cf. Emmanuel E. Etta and Asukwo Offiong, "The Reality of African Epistemology," in *International Journal of Innovative Science, Engineering & Technology*, vol. 6, 281.
[282] Etta and Offiong, *The Reality of African Epistemology*, 282.

them."[283] The embeddedness of knowledge in the hierarchy of being is such that the higher beings often provide the higher source of knowledge like God/the gods inspiring knowledge on the divinities, the divinities on the ancestors, the ancestors to humans and humans to the lower species, and so on. Though the lower beings can supply knowledge to the higher ones, but only indirectly or in reversal.

The whole chain of being therefore becomes a cyclic order of epistemic experiences and rationality within a unitary community. The epistemology of Africans is by this logic communitarian and unitary. And its unitary form incorporates forces beyond mere human sources. Humankind, therefore, is not the measure of all things in African epistemology, unlike in the Greek thoughts of Protagoras. Thus, Zubairi B. Naseem posits that "The [African] traditional epistemology does not approach the problem of knowledge by dividing its domain into the rational, empirical and mystical."[284]

This collective means of knowledge production is the reason one often hears African thoughts expressed in such social prefix as "we know," 'we think," "our people say' and not: "I know," "I think," etc. The originator of thoughts is not differentiated from his community of thought generation as seen in the Cartesian *cogito*. As Pantaleon Iroegbu explains, in African philosophy and its epistemology, knowledge is defined in contents by both an individual and a communal affair. Only individuals think because only individuals have the thinking faculty, later,

---

[283] Bert Hamming, "Epistemology from the African Point of View," January 7, 2008,1.
[284] Naseem B. Zubairi, "African Heritage and Contemporary Life: An Experience of Epistemology Change," www.cnp.orgU30T Accessed. December 20, 2008.

people bring their individual thoughts together under a community to form an epistemic harmony and synthesis for the individual and integrated good of their society.[285] Thus, one thinks in terms of the whole, and contributes his or her thoughts to the group. This is more important in society, given that the individual is defined by his or her relationship to the group.[286]

Given that African authorship of thoughts is not essentially singular, as in classical Western epistemology, the credit and even the protection of intellectual rights are not often observed. Laws are made to protect the intellectual rights of generators of ideas. This is why plagiarism is a crime. But what happens to the intellectual rights of collective thought generators in most African societies and their products which are embedded in their community thoughts and traditions? Do they share the same rights as other generators of ideas in other places of the world? What happens when a community's thought tradition is plagiarized without acknowledgment? Why are there no conventional laws protecting the collective products of intellectual rights of communities in Africa whose ideas in science and arts are often exploited and utilized by explorers, researchers, artists etc.

There are means or sources, peculiar to African epistemology. They include divine revelation, communal knowledge, oral tradition, ancestral knowledge, and mystical experiences. Apart from these, African epistemology shares other general sources of human knowledge with conventional epistemology like perception, rationality, intuition, memory, experiments, education,

---

[285] Cf. Pantaleon Iroegbu, *Enwisdomizaiton and African Philosophy* (Owerri: International Universities Ltd, 1994), 122.
[286] Cf. Etta and Offiong, "The Reality of African Epistemology," 299.

authority, etc. The passing on of information from the gods, the divinities and the ancestor to humans is considered a major source of knowledge in Africa. According to Etta and Offiong, oral tradition is another major source of knowledge in African epistemology and it deals with "a method found usually in African societies in which history, stories, folktales, myths, religion, proverbs, beliefs, songs, and rituals are transmitted from one generation to another."[287] Ancestral knowledge on the other hand in African epistemology as source of knowledge is rooted in the system's holistic ontology in which there is a bond between the living and the dead forebears of the community.[288]

Mystical knowledge also is a type of knowledge that transcends common sense knowledge, seen as a peculiar source of knowledge in African epistemology. According to Andrew Uduigwomen, mystical knowledge is a knowledge acquired exclusively by diviners, mediums, priests, native doctors, rainmakers, herbalists and so on. He posits that these people are believed to possess "innate abilities" that enable them to manipulate the spirit world and to obtain knowledge from them in favor of the natural world.[289]

African epistemology is also existential in the sense that it is shaped by the existential circumstances surrounding a truth value. It has an essentially context dependent theory of knowledge given that it takes note of the important roles of the human and societal factors in establishing any knowledge claims.[290] What this implies is

---

[287] Etta and Offiong, "The Reality of African Epistemology," 302.
[288] Cf. Etta and Offiong, "The Reality of African Epistemology," 299.
[289] Andrew Uduigwomen, "The Place of Oral Tradition in African Epistemology," in *Footmarks on African Philosophy* (Lagos: O. O. P. 1995), 38.
[290] Cf. Etta and Offiong, "The Reality of African Epistemology," 287.

that African epistemology studies knowledge considering the cultural circumstances and existential realities or worldviews of a particular people.

The existential categories of a given society shape the peculiar epistemic perception and rationality of African communities. What people experience and what affects them determine how they aspire and attain true and believable knowledge. Knowledge in African epistemology therefore does not only derive from the cognitive insight alone but obtains intuition from affective domain as seen in *Akonuche* (an epistemic concept) in Igbo epistemology. This is why the challenges and vicissitudes of life affect what many African societies accept as true and as false. It is a related pragmatic approach to truth prior to, and like the theories of truth developed by pragmatists and Instrumentalists like Sanders Peirce, William James, and John Dewey in Western epistemology.

Furthermore, Amechi Udefi writes that "the discourse of African epistemology can be subdivided into two phases: namely its early beginnings and later attempts. In its early beginnings, the scholars whose works are associated or linked with this view, were mostly religious clerics and theologians."[291] Among them include Placide Tempels, *Bantu Philosophy* (1959); E. Bolaji Idowu, Olodumare: *God in Yoruba Belief* (1962); W. E. Abraham, *The Mind of Africa* (1966); J. B. Danquah, *The Akan Doctrine of God* (1968); John S. Mbiti, *African Religions and Philosophy* (1969) etc. The main intention of these scholars was to argue that African epistemology or way of knowing flows from African ontology and theology. They apparently refute the so-called civilizing mission of the

---

[291] Udefi, "The Rationale for an African Epistemology,108.

Europeans with its dominant ideology which ascribed a pre-logical mental frame to the Africans and other non-Western peoples during the hey-day of colonialism.

Udefi remarks however, that in more recent discussions on African epistemology, we see some scholars who engage more in conceptualization and theorization on epistemic concepts, categories, and processes, which are typically African, while interpreting African peculiar experiences in the act of knowing. Here one finds scholars like Kwesi Wiredu, *The Concept of Truth*, (1978), Barry Hallen's and J. O. Sodipo's *"Knowledge, Belief and Witchcraft,"* (1986). Udefi's *Igbo Epistemology*, (2014) also falls within this category of African epistemology.

However, it is important to note as Udefi indicates that the scholarship of these intellectuals have broadly divided African epistemologists into the Universalists and the Particularists. The former are pro-analytic in their reflections and argue that epistemology is universal and does not need to be racially or ethnically defined. The latter group who are more existentialistic in approach hold that though philosophy is universal, yet lived experiences of every society give them a unique mindset and differentiation as seen in African epistemology.[292] For the latter group, this peculiarity is part of why we have classification in philosophy that are based on geo-regional inclination. Thus, if we can talk of Greek philosophy, British Empiricism, French Existentialism and German idealism, speaking of African epistemology or Igbo epistemology would not be inconsistent with ways of

---

[292] Cf. Amechi Udefi, "Theoretical Foundations for an African Epistemology" in *Footprints in Philosophy,* ed. R. A. Akanmidu (Ibadan: Hope Publications Ltd, 2005), 74.

identification or classification of peculiar areas of philosophy.

Udefi maintains a moderate ground in the face of this polarization, to which I subscribe. His reason is that there is no dogmatic domain in African epistemology since there are elements of the universalist and the particularist perspectives in most African epistemological discourses. In his *The Rationale for an African Epistemology: A Critical Examination of the Igbo Views on Knowledge, Belief, and Justification*, he made efforts to use his reflections on Igbo epistemology (an aspect of African epistemology) to demonstrate this stance. His reflections on Igbo epistemology are what inspired my analytic discussions on the epistemic concept of *akonuche*.

10.5 *Akonuche* in Igbo Epistemology

In his reflections on the epistemology of the Igbo people in Nigeria,[293] Udefi remarks that,

> Igbo epistemology...is not in contradiction or opposition with Western epistemology. In every epistemological system or study, one is bound to find such core notions as 'knowledge, justification, truth, belief, ideas, intentions, explanation, understanding, experience and human action' etc. One term which encapsulates all these is rationality which again is found, in one way or the other, in all societies and conceptual systems. Igbo thought is no exception to this, since they attempt to

---

[293] The Igbo people is an ethnic group in the South-East Nigeria, sometimes called the people of Biafra.

validate their knowledge following certain epistemological cannons as found elsewhere.[294]

His epistemology delved into an analysis of two Igbo epistemic terms: '*amamife*' and '*nchekwube*,'[295] which putatively translate 'knowledge' and 'belief' in English. Thus, "*amamife* (knowledge), according to him, is used by the Igbo "to explain those things or events for which they have good reasons, and which can be verified through common sense perception or observation." [296] Here, "justification is based on perception which is obtained through the five senses. So, when the Igbo say *ihe mfuru na anya ma uche kwado kwa ya* (What I see with my eyes and which my mind or consciousness supports), then they can claim to know it."[297] *Nchekwube/nkwenye* (belief) on the other hand, according to him, is used by the Igbo to express those things which they accept on trust and confidence for which there is reliability or certainty. In that case, the object of consciousness at such epistemic status still requires justification to be accepted as truth. Justification for *nchekwube/nkwenye* (belief) to become *eziokwu* (truth) can come through testimony or reports from persons, especially *ndichie* (elders), *Ozo* (titled holders) and *dibia afa* (native diviners/doctors),[298] whose account are taken as true and

---

[294] Udefi, "The Rationale for an African Epistemology, 114.
[295] I do not subscribe to Udefi's translation of *nchekwube* (belief) in this context. Nchekwube is more in line with belief in religious context. A more epistemological translation of belief in Igbo epistemology in my opinion would be *nkwenye* or *okwukwe*.
[296] Udefi, "The Rationale for an African Epistemology, 114.
[297] Udefi, "The Rationale for an African Epistemology, 114.
[298] Elders, Ozo titled men and diviners are regarded as persons of honesty and integrity, not just by their personal intelligence but also by their cultic roles in the society as mediators with the divine, and whose roles oblige them to always tell the truth. Their testimonies are very

reliable.[299] Thus, justification is anchored on the authority of consultation with trusted authorities than personal experimentation as seen in some analytic and pragmatic western epistemologies.

Udefi equally analyzes inductive reasoning in Igbo epistemology. He writes that

> By inductive inference in Western philosophy, it is meant a procedure in logical and scientific research in which we make judgment concerning a phenomenon or event from a mere observation of a particular fact to a conclusion covering many instances or cases…. [on the contrary] the Igbo believe that past experiences provide sufficient ground to infer what will happen now and in the future.[300]

The inference from past or residue of thought is sufficient in Igbo epistemology to draw logical conclusion. Inductive reasoning in Igbo epistemology, therefore, hinges on a combination of coherence theory with past events, correspondence theory with concrete or social reality, consensus theory with community opinion and relativist theory given that what is acceptably true may be relative to a peculiar community where such truth has pragmatic value. These epistemic concepts and processes constitute the essential elements of Igbo epistemology according to Udefi.

In Igbo epistemology, the holistic experiential encounter with intelligible object commences cognitive awareness, starting from exterior encounter /experience, which is not only subjective but united in the forces of nature as indicated earlier about the holistic ontology of the

---

reliable over what they attest to, and where they are ignorant of something, they have same obligation to acknowledge that.
[299] Cf. Udefi, "The Rationale for an African Epistemology, 114.
[300] Cf. Udefi, "The Rationale for an African Epistemology, 114.

African personality. The knower becomes aware by his sensation, perception, beliefs and even feelings in the exterior objects of experience. One may make a faint and unjustified claim to knowledge in this initial encounter merely by sight (*ihe m ji anya m fu*), by hearing (*ihe m ji nti m nu*), by trust (*ihe m gbadoro ukwu*), by grasp (*ihe m ji aka*), by feeling (*ihe metutara m*) or by belief (*ihe m kwenyere*).

Sometimes, the experiential operation may involve the mystical, that is, experience of revelation beyond the senses (*ihe e kpughere m*). The mystical experience on a knower comes from intuition or spiritual forces of nature through ancestral connection or spirit of God, and it is seen as potential knowledge among the Igbo. It provides a truth possibility, subject to discernment. Igbo epistemology holistically embraces the sensitive, the inner consciousness, the voluntary, and the spiritual in the experiential apprehension of object of immediate encounter. At this experiential apprehension, one can avow that one knows a particular thing, material, mental or mystical by saying *ama m ya*, (I know it, him, her), *a ma m maka ya* (I know about it, him, or her). But this still does not establish a justified true belief in Igbo epistemology.

Knowledge at this simple awareness still requires further justification, which is why I can attest of something without full comprehension when I say: *a ma m ya, ma na amachaghi m ya ofuma/ ama m ya, mana o ka folu* (I know it, but I do not fully understand it). Thus, reserving a space for fuller understanding. I can say: *ama m ya/maka ya, mana a ghotachabeghi m ya* (I know about it, but I have not yet understood it). What it means is that I may have known something without proper understanding or insight of it. One will still need further explanations (*nkowa*) to attain a higher comprehension/truth (*eziokwu di na ya*) of the issue already perceived. Proper achievement of understanding in Igbo epistemology becomes possible through a combination of elements of correspondence, coherence, and consensus theories of truth as mentioned earlier. This is achieved through a collaboration of epistemic experiences with social collaboration in comprehension. Thus, an achievement of insight is not often a singular authorship among the Igbo. It is rather a product and property of collective insight, which is why authorship of thought is not prefixed by: "I think," or "I know," but "we think" (*anyi chere*) or "we know (*anyi mara)*. The product of such collective consciousness, if it agrees with the consensus of understanding of the society, that is, what is generally accepted as true, becomes what the Igbo call *amamife* or *ako* (it is a form of understanding based on propositional, logical, or functional/know-how cognition).

Amamife satisfies the achievement of truth (*eziokwu*) at propositional, logical, and functional levels. When somebody possesses the understanding in dealing with dialogical issues, logical coherence, and technical know-how, we say: *O mara ife* or *O mara ako* (he knows something). It is important that a further morphological analysis of the term *ima-ako* (different from *ima-ife*), can in some circumstances refer to knowledge of the negative techniques and logical propositions that assist what may not be ethically satisfying. *Ima-ako* over and above being a form of cognition can specifically imply a negative cognition like cunningness, logical scheming, stinginess, or meanness.

Ima-ako might often identify with smartness for survival or functionality, which might not respect ethical interiority or moral demands. This is part of why *ima-ako* or even *ima-ife* does not yet make one's knowledge complete, neither will having such knowledge make people repose an epistemic authenticity on a person. One could be regarded as intelligent, smart, or savvy but not fully knowledgeable. A full comprehensive knowledge in Igbo epistemology is what they call: *Akonuche*.

Akonuche is an epistemic concept and a composite term from *ako/amamife* (cognitive intelligence) and *uche* (volitive wisdom). Further details of these significant terms are relevant here. Sequel to above, *ako*/amamife dwells in the domain of sensitive and intellective cognition. Udefi explains that,

> The term 'amamife' is used to refer to knowledge. Knowledge so conceived is restricted to those things, or events for which one can offer good reason, and which can be verified through sense perception and observation. Hence, when the Igbos say: *ihe mfuru na anya ma uche kwado kwa ya* (what I see with my eyes and which my mind, or consciousness supports), they are alluding to [this form of] knowledge.[301]

Ima ife or *Ima ako* (to know something) connotes knowledge that is based on sense and rational cognition. It is not just achieved by empirical and rational sources but by methodologies and explanations or education. It is a type of knowledge that is in the realm of the intellective and the functional understanding of things, people, situations, logic, or propositions. *Ako* has to do with ability of intelligent expression, perceptive power, propositional knowledge, logical smartness, science or social savvy, social functionality etc. It is a **learned capacity** of dexterity and cleverness, through education/teaching, training,

---

[301] Udefi, "The Rationale for an African Epistemology, 114.

instruction, socialization and apprenticeship of technicality and logic. Thus, the popular saying among the Igbo: *akuziere nwata, o mara ako* or *ife* (when a child is taught, he knows). But fullness of knowledge is not limited in this concept. Fullness of knowledge would require, not just these acts of the senses and the intellect but act of the will (*uche*).

Uche is the act of the mind in the realm of the faculty and operations of the will. It is the voluntarist version of the operation of the human mind, not really at the pure cognitive domain but the volitive domain, though it needs to be enlightened by the intellective faculty. This relates to the Thomistic differentiation of the faculties of the soul into the intellective and the volitive.[302]

In his differentiation of the faculties of the mind, Aquinas identifies the intellect, according to J.A. West, as "the capacity for understanding and thought, or a power of apprehension and knowing."[303] Claudia Eisen-Murphy calls it "the rational agent's cognitive power."[304] On the other hand, she explains that for Aquinas, the will is "an innate positive inclination towards the good. It is that aspect of a rational agent which disposes her to pursue what she considers good."[305] This differentiation, with its practical implications for our understanding of the mind, is a significant contribution to philosophical thought. This is why Anthony Kenny writes that "the will is the power to

---

[302] Cf. Aquinas, *Summa Theologica* 1, q.82, a. 4. c.
[303] J. A. West, "Aquinas on Intellect, Will, and Faith," in *Aporia* Vol. 13 number 1.
[304] Claudia Eisen-Murphy, "Aquinas on Voluntary Beliefs," *American Catholic Philosophical Quarterly*, Fall 2000, 74(4): 576.
[305] Eisen-Murphy, "Aquinas on Voluntary Beliefs," 576.

have wants which only the intellect can frame."³⁰⁶ This concept underscores the dynamic relationship between the intellect and the will, a key area of interest in philosophical and theological studies. In this sense, the intellect moves the will, not as an efficient cause but rather as a final cause, since whatever is perceived by the intellect as good moves the will as an end.³⁰⁷ Nevertheless, Aquinas also holds that the will can move the intellect by efficient causation.³⁰⁸

Uche therefore is the will intending the good as enlightened by the intellect *ako/amamife*. However, the freedom of the will is such that one can, therefore, choose to apply the will for negative ends as *ajo-uche/ajo-obi* (badwill) or *ezi-uche/ezi-obi* (positive end/goodwill) according to Igbo epistemology. If one applies the will for a negative end, one's cognitive faculty is judged vitiated and corrupt, and this could imply an inherent denial of *uche* in the knower (as deliberate or radical unintelligibility). People could say: *O mara ako, mana onweghi uche / o mara ako mana onweghi ezi obi* (he knows something, but he lacks true knowledge or good will/conscience). The perfection of cognition is rather achieved when one applies one's cognitive conclusion to positive volitive ends (goodwill).

When cognition is mediated by goodwill, one is then operating with *uche,* which implies the act of the soul/will desiring the good of its intentional object. People can say of the person: *onwere uche* (he has goodwill [with thoughtfulness/knowledge]). And to achieve this would mean that one has judged his/her choices of action, after it has been enlightened in the previous levels of cognition to make this decision for the right course of action. To exercise

---

³⁰⁶ Anthony Kenny, *Aquinas on Mind* (New York: Routledge, 1993), 59.
³⁰⁷ Cf. Aquinas, *Summa Theologica* 1, q.82, a. 4. c.
³⁰⁸ Cf. Kenny, *Aquinas on Mind*, 59.

goodwill assumes an enlightened mind, which shows that in Igbo epistemology, choosing the right action is not something done impulsively or ignorantly. It is the habit of making the right decision and taking correct action which emanates from an enlightened mind. It implies arriving at an epistemic climax where cognition meets volition (goodwill), thus, forming goodwill in cognition. *Inwe uche* (having goodwilled–cognition), produces a habit of conscientious intelligence termed *Akonuche*.[309]

Akonuche is a synthetic terminology where *ako* (perceptive and intelligent cognition) *na* (and) *uche /obioma* (goodwill/thoughtfulness/conscience) form an integrated order involving a synthesis of epistemology and ethics. It is related to the biblical concept of wisdom as a higher level of knowledge which is not limited to the knowledge of the empirical things.[310] To have *akonuche* is a **cultivated habit** and not just a **learned capacity**, and the habit must have a balance of intelligence and goodwill and must be such that true wisdom is achieved. It is the moral mediation of intelligence with meaning and conscience.

---

[309] *Ako* means "cognition", *na* means "and", *uche* means "goodwill/conscience". *Akonuche* literally means "knowledge with goodwill/conscience."

[310] Biblical literature tries to differentiate three levels of knowledge. Experiential knowledge of facts and information about things, termed *gnosis* in Greek (Romans 15:14), Intelligent understanding in practical action and good judgement in decision, called *phronesis* in Greek (Eph 1:8), and Wisdom known as *Sophia* in Greek, which refers to highest level of knowledge and has to do with skilled discernment and pure insight (Wisdom 7:22-27). This also relates to Aristotle's three levels of knowledge: *theoria*, *episteme* and *sophia*. Cf. Nigel Rooms, "Paul as Practical Theologian: *Phronesis* in Philippians," in *Practical Theology*, 5.1 (2012): 81ff, Published online: 21 Apr 2015.

Obododimma Oha writing on an Igbo philosophical journal, *Eke na Egwurugwu*, on "Where Is Ako, Where Is Uche?" explains that

> *Akonauche* (sometimes written as '*akonuuche*' to reflect what, in phonology is called a feature smear, the attribute of one sound affecting the sound of its neighbour) is an Igbo compound word formed from '*ako*' (being wary, cleverness, discerning, cautious) and '*uche*' (thoughtfulness, wisdom, etc.). Both are obviously relatives, and, in recognition of this affinity, the Igbo put them together to form a mega-term that we can translate as a soundness of mind from which somebody critically looks at an issue and makes the right choices.[311]

Oha in this explanation provides an insight to the fact that *ako* is relative to cognitive capacity for cleverness, carefulness, social understanding, empirical comprehension, technicality in existential issues, logical smartness, and ability to satisfy the demands of basic insight, understanding and judgement on real life issues. But *uche* would require more than these attributes of *ako*. *Uche* will demand deeper thoughts, wisdom, discernment, and responsible decisions. One who possesses this epistemic synthesis is said to have *akonuche (onye nwere akonuche)*, and he or she is the one taken to have true or complete knowledge of things or situation. He or she is seen as a truly knowledgeable person (*onye mara ife nwekwa uche*).

Of course, some earlier translations of Igbo language have rendered *amamife* as wisdom, but the right translation of wisdom in its epistemological import should be *akonuche*, which is excellent or comprehensive knowledge,

---

[311] Obododimma Oha, "Where Is *Ako*; where Is *Uche*? in *Eke na Egwurugwu*, November 17, 2018, https://obododimma-oha.blogspot.com/2018/11/where-is-ako-where-is-uche.html?m1.

and as such wisdom. Oha in his reflections on *akonuche* seems to have slipped into this translation misconception when he tries to identify wisdom with *amamife*, (and not *akonuche*). However, he then gets trapped in the crisis of clarification when he alludes at the same time that *amamife* is a subordinate term to *akonuche*. Thus, if he means that *akonuche* is "a superordinate where we could locate such terms as *amamiihe* (**wisdom**/intelligent cognition), *nghota* (understanding), *itughari uche* (reasoning), etc,"[312] it implies that *amamife* is deductively lower in epistemic hierarchy than *akanuche*. And where wisdom is the highest realm of epistemic transcendence in Igbo epistemology, it should translate as *akonuche* which is the "superordinate" and optimal dimension of epistemic expression.

Amamife as a "subordinate" to *akonuche* (superordinate) should logically belong to the lower order of cognitive realm alongside understanding (*nghota*), and reasoning (*itughari uche*) as he rightly mentioned.[313] *Akonuche* incorporates and sublimates *amamife*, *nghota* and *itughari uche*, where one is not only expected to achieve right judgement but to have enlightened insight to decide with goodwill. Cultivating honesty and goodwill through insight at the cognitive steps prior to *akonuche* is one of the essential requirements for achieving *akonuche*. Acting from goodwill is a sign of an enlightened mind in Igbo epistemology.

If one acts contrary to goodwill, in that case, acting from bad will, he or she is still taken to be without proper insight. To have cognition with bad will is not esteemed in

---

[312] Oha, "Where Is *Ako*; where Is *Uche*?" 1.
[313] Cf. Oha, "Where Is *Ako*, where Is *Uche*? 1.

Igbo epistemology. Thus, one could be said to have understanding but lacks conscience. Such a learned (bad-willed) person is not seen to possess wisdom. But one who possesses it (*onye nwere akonuche*) cannot be said to lack neither goodwill nor correct cognition, expressed in perception or intellection. It is pertinent to cite what Oha explains in this regard that,

> The term *akonauche* is sometimes clipped in Igbo discourse and used simply as '*uche*' (even though the word '*uche*' also exists as a free morpheme used in the language). In that case, it is assumed that the interlocutor has competence enough in the language to recover the removed part, '*ako+na.*'...*Uche* tells us the person is just not talking about the possession of wisdom or not, [that] caution or cleverness is entailed in it. Otherwise, how can one be wise if one is not equally cautious and [intelligent]?[314]

Therefore, to have *akonuche* would also imply being an intelligent and truthful or honest person. That is the true measure of a knowledgeable person. Udefi in this light posits that,

> the Igbo would not refer to *onye asi* (a liar) as knowledgeable and the reason is that both knowledge and truth are regarded as possessing divine and moral status. This is in keeping with their saying, *ezi-okwu bu ndu* (truth is life). So, in order to verify the truth of a claim or event, it is not enough to see how propositions correspond with facts or the weight of superior logic of the argument, but it is important to consider the person's *omume* (moral character), that is, his moral standing within the community is paramount.[315]

---

[314] Oha, "Where Is *Ako*; where Is *Uche*?" 1.
[315] Udefi, "The Rationale for an African Epistemology," 115.

Akonuche is not just learnt, it is acquired as a habit of epistemology and ethics. One knows something truly and justifiably, only if he or she also possesses wisdom (*akonuche*). *Akonuche* is integrative and comprehensive of cognition and conscience in the act of knowing and meaning. One who possesses it is expected, not only to know, but to responsibly decide and act according to the conscientious conclusions of his insight. To have perceptive, intelligent, and rational/logical knowledge, either as propositional, technical, functional, or social knowledge, (*ima ife/ima ako*), without goodwill (*ezi uche/ezi obi*), conscientious knowing, moral cognition, intelligent responsibility, is tantamount to having a mitigated, corrupt, and incomplete knowledge in Igbo epistemology.

Furthermore, the empirical and the rational segments of act of knowing which are in the domain of the operative faculties of the intellect are technically and socially learned. But the moral and conscientious segments which are in the domain of the operative acts of the (goodwill/conscience) will are not just learned but appropriated through personal commitment, refinement of character, civilization of thoughts and responsible decision to be good in understanding. A person may be literate, learned, and intelligent, and will still be regarded as without true knowledge (*onye enweghi uche*) if he or she lacks moral character in Igbo epistemology. Same goes for someone who is unintelligent or worse still, who accompanies his or her corrupt intelligence with bad or dysfunctional actions. People can say that "*oma ako mana o machaghi ihe/ onwecheghi uche*"-he or she knows, or he or she is smart or savvy but he or she knows *nothing* still (given his bad-will). *Nothing* in this context implies absence of goodwill and conscience. Bad-will or evil therefore does reduce even intelligence to nothingness in Igbo epistemology.

Chapter Eleven: Recent Topics in Epistemology

11.1 Current Issues in Epistemology

As the study of human knowledge continues to evolve, there are new concepts and developments that arise in the process. In the contemporary epoch, which is very much aided by globalization and innovative technologies, there are emerging issues and events of the human scholarship and society which have become critical concerns for epistemology too. For instance, agnotology and post-truth mentality draw the attention of epistemology today. Furthermore, new waves of knowing in the use of artificial intelligence has also changed the curriculum of epistemology as we must now have a difference between machine thinking and human thinking in the act of cognition or knowing. These are the current and relevant themes in epistemology we shall briefly introduce in this section for further research and studies in future.

11.2 Agnotology

Epistemology is aimed at providing justification for human knowledge by questioning its assumptions. However, while this effort is made in the pursuance and preservation of truth, some intelligent efforts are sometimes made by some people to fight the same truth, especially where truth conflicts with a particular interest of the persons in the project. Education in the contemporary age is no longer presumed to be for the pursuance of the truth. There are also forms of education aimed at producing ignorance for a specific purpose. Studies in social epistemology show that there are efforts to deliberately induce ignorance by some scholars, to prevent certain elements of truth for some specific reasons or interest. The study of these efforts is today identified by social epistemologists as agnotology. Andrian Kreye explains that agnotology has to do with the study of deliberate, culturally induced ignorance or doubt, typically to sell a product, influence opinion, or win favor, particularly through the publication of inaccurate or misleading scientific data (disinformation).[316]

Recent studies and insight in epistemology reveal that there are some reasons that make people to embark in the invention and production of untruth, lies, fake facts and to work towards the promotion of ignorance or misinformation which enhances their own advantages. Some of the reasons often invoked in this interest are state security and business interest. The state can reserve or suppress certain truths for military classified information or intelligence. Some corporations can distort certain facts and evidence to protect their business interests and profit too.

Other means that enable agnotology include media manipulation, secrecy, suppression of some relevant information, destruction of documents, and selective memory or confirmation bias, whereby there is a tendency to search for, interpret, favor, and recall information in a way that confirms or supports one's prior beliefs or values.[317] Most times, agnotology is sustained by some other epistemic forms of anti-intellectualism like conspiracy of silence, cognitronics, cognitive inertia, cognitive dissonance, denialism, obscurantism, historical

---

[316] Cf. Andrian Kreye, "We Will Overcome Agnotology (The Cultural Production of Ignorance," in *The Edge World Question Center 2007*, 6.
[317] Cf. Raymond S. Nickerson, "Confirmation bias: A Ubiquitous Phenomenon in Many Guises," *Review of General Psychology*, **2** (2) (1998): 175.

negationism, junk science, anti-science, misinformation, disinformation and so on.

Karen W. Arenson on agnotology observes that there is a "culturally" induced ignorance or doubt, through deliberate publications of inaccurate or misleading scientific data. [318] Robert N. Proctor posits that "agnotology," is the deliberate attempt by persons, corporations, and governments to manufacture, sell, spread, and advance ignorance for some specific reasons or interests. The origin of the term is traceable to Proctor in his 1995 book, *The Cancer Wars: How Politics Shapes What We Know and Don't Know About Cancer*. There, he explains that,

> Historians and philosophers of science have tended to treat ignorance as an ever-expanding vacuum into which knowledge is sucked – or even, as Johannes Kepler once put it, as the mother who must die for science to be born. Ignorance, though, is more complex than this. It has a distinct and changing political geography that is often an excellent indicator of the politics of knowledge. We need political *agnotology* to complement our political epistemologies.[319]

Georgina Kenyon remarks that agnotology is "the study of willful acts to spread confusion and deceit, usually to sell a product or win favor."[320] The logic of agnotology is that ignorance is power in the hands of powerful institutions who deliberately create ignorance and

---

[318] Cf. K.W. Arenson, "What Organizations Don't Want to Know Can Hurt" In *The New York Times*, 22nd August 2006.
[319] Robert Proctor, *Cancer Wars: How Politics Shapes What We Know and Don't Know About Cancer* (New York: Basic Books, 1995), 8.
[320] Georgina Kenyon, "The Man Who Studies the Spread of Ignorance," in *BBC-Future News*, 6th January 2017.

widespread doubt as ploy of dominance of public knowledge. Thus, ignorance is not just the "not-yet-known," it is also a political ploy, by powerful agents who want you "not to know." [321] Here, the body responsible for deliberate spread of ignorance is likely to use its methods to inhibit, suppress, destroy, and manipulate objective facts and data on issues that affect their interest. Agnotology is an effort in social construction of ignorance for an effective interest and use.

Robert N. Proctor and Londa Schiebinger in their 2008 publication, *Agnotology: The Making and Unmaking of Ignorance*, have tried to provide insight on this reflection by raising critical epistemological question: "why don't we know what we don't know?"[322] This is a more challenging question than the traditional epistemological ones, where we are often concerned with question of how we know and what we know to be true. Are there things we do not know yet, and why do we not yet know them? Is ignorance always an absence of knowledge or an outcome of cultural and political manipulation in which we are victims? What is the goal of those who promote ignorance? Is ignorance as good as knowledge, especially where both may have functional values? Is there no difference between my knowledge and your ignorance? Or is my ignorance as good as your knowledge?

Attending to these questions are the challenging issues facing epistemological studies today. How do we develop a new method of epistemology that can tackle these new developments in the effort to stop thoughts that deviate

---

[321] Cf. Kenyon, The Man Who Studies the Spread of Ignorance,
[322] Robert N. Proctor and Londa Schiebinger, eds. *Agnotology: The Making and Unmaking of Ignorance* (Stanford: Stanford University Press, 2008), 90.

objectivity and manipulate truth? It is relevant that epistemology must widen its horizon of research to address these emerging issues. It must develop methods to understand what we know and to search for what we know not. The critical study of human knowledge must broaden its scope and develop more sophisticated approaches to knowledge in the face of denialist's dimensions in how we obtain and manage human knowledge in the new world order. Deeper studies on how we are made not to know (agnotology) should be a serious dimension of epistemology today.

11.3 Post-Truth Phenomenon

A recent development in human knowledge and its relation to truth in epistemology is the phenomenon of post-truth.[323] It refers to an epistemic attitude to reality in which objective facts and logical reasons are less influential in people deciding on public opinion than appeals to emotion and personal belief.[324] The lexicology of post-truth is very recent, having been introduced into the English lexicon just recently. It is about people's deliberate response and disposition to accept and live with untruth when it suits their psychological tranquility. Its historical etymology is traceable to the words of the Serbian American playwright, Steve Tesich, who in his 1992 article, "A Government of Lies" used the term while criticizing the American public

---

[323] In post-truth phenomenon, people anchor on their beliefs and emotions in accepting something to be true rather than using reason and facts. They can create "alternative facts" in place of the real facts, for as long as they might favour their interest.

[324] The prefix "post" here is not much about the sense of "after". It is about an atmosphere in which an idea is considered irrelevant even in the face of its facts and reason.

for submissive acceptance of the lies of some of her governments. He mentioned such cases like the scandals of Watergate (1972-1974), Iran-Contra (1985-1987) and Persian Gulf War (1990-1991). He writes: "we, as a free people, have freely decided that we want to live in some post-truth world."[325] And in reference to the administration of President Bush senior, he writes that Americans have decided to consciously live in a "post-truth" world.[326]

By 2004, the term resurfaced in the work of Ralph Keyes, *The Post-Truth Era.*[327] In this book he argues that we do not just have truth and lies in epistemology, but a third category of ambiguous statements, that are not exactly true but at the same time do fall short of a lie. This implies that truth and lies are no longer absolutes in a post-truth order but are mutable and fluid and can be fantasized to suit our emotional acceptance. Truth, therefore, can change face, just like lies can, and one could choose which of them suits a situation for pragmatic ends, especially in politics. Thus, we have a new political notion termed "post-truth politics," in political science today.

Post-truth as an epistemic phenomenon is not only recent, but has become very influential and dominant, that it was voted the "word of the year" in 2016 by the Oxford Dictionaries. This is based on its prevalent political impact in the Presidential election of Donald Trump in the United States and the Brexit referendum in United Kingdom.

---

[325] Richard Kreitner, "Post-Truth and Its Consequences: What a 25-Year-Old Essay Tells Us About the Current Moment," in *The Nation*. 30 November 2016, Retrieved 1 December 2016.
[326] Cf. Steve Tesich, "A Government of Lies," *The Nation*, January 6, 1992.
[327] Cf. Ralph Keyes, *The Post-Truth Era: Dishonesty and Deception in Contemporary Life* (New York: St. Martin's Press, 2004).

Oxford dictionaries define post-truth as "a term relating to or denoting circumstances in which objective facts are less influential in shaping public opinion than appeals to emotion and personal belief."[328] In this case, the once epistemic clear and distinct line between truth and lie is bridged by a middle ground which is neither truth nor lie. Keyes have given it such descriptions as "enhanced truth" "neo-truth," "soft truth,' "faux truth," and "truth lite."[329]

Of course, prior to the coinage and popular use of the term, post-truth phenomenon as a political epistemology had always been shown in some scholarly writings. In the ancient Greek philosophy, Plato in one of the Socratic dialogues, *The Republic*, had to battle playwrights and poets who opposed the philosopher king that has concrete knowledge and truth. These Playwrights and poets distract people from the truth, and instead feed them with fabrications. They are like the post-truth tellers of our age. By mid-20th century, George Orwell in his *Politics and English Language*, had maintained that politicians generally lie and make their lies sound truthful. He writes that "Political language – and, with variations, this is true of all political parties, from conservatives to anarchists – is designed to make lies sound truthful and murder the respectable, and to give an appearance of solidity to pure wind."[330]

---

[328] Oxford Dictionary, s.v. "Word of the Year 2016," 2016, https://en.oxforddictionaries.com/word-of-the-year/word-of-the-year-2016.
[329] Cf. Ralph Keyes, *The Post-Truth Era: Dishonesty and Deception in Contemporary Life* (New York: St. Martin's Press, 2004), 1.
[330] George Orwell, *Politics, and the English Language* (Peterborough: Broadview Press, 2006), 258.

In 1967, Hannah Arendt in the article "Truth and Politics" in *The New Yorker* argues that truthfulness and honesty have never been counted among the virtues of politicians, and that they have always used lies as necessary and justifiable instruments in their operations as politicians and statesmen.[331] She argues further that the greatest enemy to factual truth is an opinion, and not even lies, especially in light of current predilection of politicians to blur fact and opinion. This epistemic stance which people often call their opinion, and not really a lie, which is its proper name is enhanced by freedom of expression and right of interpretation or perspectives that form part of a democratic society. Freedom of expression, especially through the mass media, in a democratic setting can lead to a manipulation of concepts like interpretation, perspectives, opinion, facts, fancy, and fabrication in the effort to blur the distinct dividing line between truth and lie. The result is that the public is left confused at times, or they deliberately opt for what feeds their sentiment, and it becomes difficult for them to differentiate between fact, fabrication, opinion, lie and truth. This phenomenon is the reason sometimes, those who speak the truth in public are branded public enemies, while the manipulators of facts are honored as patriots and friends of society. In these thoughts, therefore, the phenomenon of post-truth was already born before its vocabulary was invented in the social sciences.

Philosophers and social scientists have tried to identify the plausible causes of post-truth phenomenon in politics. There are some who think that post-modernism is a major influence of post-truth mentality. Part of the reason being that post-truth phenomenon has a post-modernist

---

[331] Cf. Hannah Arendt, "Truth and Politics," *The New Yorker*, February 25, 1967.

coloration that makes it somehow subtly appealing. Scholars like Matthew d'Ancona have argued that the post-truth phenomenon is rooted in post-modernist philosophy.[332] This is based on the argument that post-modernist philosophy often rejects single objective truth in favor of a multitude of subjective and relative truths. Post-modernism argues that there is no single true scientific theory or meta-narrative; rather, we have many theories and narratives fashioned from a variety of perspectives, of which none take precedence over the other. If then there is no single meaning to an issue or if one interpretation is not more correct than others, then the conclusion is that there is no single objective truth. It implies that each person has his own value, story, belief, opinion, and subjective interpretation of reality, whereby profession of truth only reflects the political ideology of an author.[333]

Post-modernist philosophy thrives on social constructivism in which both science and arts are seen to have no single meta-narrative. Scientific truth for this school of thought depends on subjective perspectives. Bruno Latour, who represents this movement, believes that science also has no single meta-narrative, and that scientific truth depends on a subjective perspective. Thus, it is basically not a product of objective facts alone, but rather, of scientific enterprise as a social enterprise, which is financed and guided by political ideologies and motives.[334] But as Arendt would argue, even if the facts cannot be known without some degree of interpretation, and without allowing for perspectives, it must be such that the facts

---

[332] Cf. Matthew d'Ancona, *Post-Truth: The New War on Truth and How to Fight Back* (London: Ebury Press, 2017), 91.
[333] Cf. Lee McIntyre, *Post-Truth* (Cambridge: MIT Press, 2018), 125.
[334] Cf. McIntyre, *Post-Truth*, 128.

cannot be altered.[335] Subjective opinion without respecting the facts will be a threat to scientific objectivity, critical thinking, and the basic idea that our opinions and beliefs should be based on factual evidence.

Even though post-modernism may not be considered as a necessary condition for the emergence of post-truth phenomenon, it must be seen to have impact on the formation of the phenomenon. It may not have rejected facts and reality as seen in post-truth epistemology, but it laid the epistemic foundations that produced it. Such foundations include casting doubt on objectivity and absoluteness of truth, legitimization of populistic points of view, and the propagation of "anything goes" or "this is my truth" version of epistemology. These sowed the seed of post-truth phenomenon.

Furthermore, there are other factors that are identified with the emergence of post-truth phenomenon. Information explosion, new disruptive media, public relations mechanics and dwindling of faith in institutions that represent truth telling are among the main ones. There is so much information in circulation as generated by the internet culture. And sometimes, overdose of information or data could bring confusion on the choice of data to be accepted as true. Sometimes similar data to the real ones are combined and made viral by innovative technology means which can render one's assessment or justification of a proposition poor.

There is also the mistrust of traditional sources of information like the conventional media, which renders careless and emotionally charged positions attractive. This happens more when they offer alternative perspectives and

---

[335] Cf. Arendt, "*Truth and Politics.*"

new dimensions outside the conventional realm. Public relations agents often capitalize on the mistrust of the conventional media to create images of things that are much more visible than the real situation of things. They make images and fabrications substitute reality in their presentations, tapping on what people hope for or what is of interest to them. They can use social media to twist facts to suit their purpose, and in some cases, amplify prejudice, provide distraction, and make real facts, especially where they are inconvenient, less attractive, and less welcoming.

Post-truth is not actually a clear lie, but something that is more subtle and deeper than lie. A liar for instance might know that he or she is lying and may deliberately be lying to conceal the truth, given at least that he or she can differentiate between truth and falsehood. But a post-truth speaker does not recognize this differentiation and as such will reject the difference between truth and falsehood. He or she would not care about whether what he or she is saying is true or not. He or she remains steadfast in his or her stance, even in the face of facts and reasons that refute his or her position. This inability of the agents of post-truth to recognize a differentiation between truth and lie is the main theme of Harry Frankfurt in his book, *On Bullshit*.[336] Frankfurt argues that the agent of post-truth, whom he calls the *Bullshitter*, is worse than a lair in epistemological judgement. The *Bullshitter* does not care whether his statements have an epistemological value or not. He simply remains indifferent to truth and lie, in speaking to his audience.[337]

---

[336] Cf. Harry G. Frankfurt, *On Bullshit* (Princeton: Princeton University Press, 1986).
[337] Cf. Frankfurt, *On Bullshit*, 55.

Knowledge and Truth

Lee McIntyre posits that the problem of post-truth phenomenon is not in the denial of the existence of truth and facts, but rather in the non-recognition of the difference and deliberate subjugation of facts to personal preconceptions and a subjective perspective. According to him, post truth speaker makes some facts more important than others, and the criterion for this depends on the extent that the fact concurs with his or her opinion and his or her prejudiced perspective. Yuval Harari further argues that fake news is as old as humanity, that what is new about post-truth is that it has been assisted by information technology, whereby trolls and hackers use big data algorithms to identify people's unique weaknesses and tendencies and then fabricate stories consistent with them. Digital technology can use stories likable by people to reinforce the prejudices of people and therefrom make them believable or accepted.[338]

The main epistemological tragedy of post-truth in the world today is not just the familiar dishonesty of some people like the politicians, but rather, the response of the public who find lies normal and comfortable. Furthermore, post-truth uses emotions to threaten rational thinking and constructive skepticism. It uses scorn to harass science, thereby destroying truth as an epistemic and moral value for social construction and progress. In a post-truth order, honest people are harassed with fake data, while experts are perceived as charlatans rather than sources of reliable knowledge and truth. In a post-truth era, biased interpretations and subjective emotional narratives substitute objective facts and apparent reason. And post-truth agents are not ignorant of the facts. They know the

---

[338] Cf. Yuval Noah Harari, "Yuval Noah Harari Extract: 'Humans are a Post-Truth Species,'" *The Observer*, August 5, 2018.

facts but make decisions to ignore or reject them, accepting rather more emotionally appealing messages. Thus, emotions trump over facts, and people are prepared to live with the effects. This is dangerous to the honesty needed in building a reliable society, and this is what Pope Francis warned the world about in March 2017, while addressing the EU leaders. He said that the world must "avoid using emotions to gain consensus."[339] These are among the reasons the post-truth phenomenon is a big concern in epistemology today.

11.4 Artificial Intelligence (AI)

The first tool in the study of human knowledge is the human mind, which produces human intelligence. In the wake of advanced information technology, otherwise called digital culture, the operation of human intelligence is now extended and sometimes, outsourced to non-human intelligence. Generation of intelligence can today be outsourced to machines, outside the human brain. This new development is changing the way we understand the human knowledge and the process of its generation. Even though formal epistemology, using computability theory, may have expected the possibility of such emergence, the fact still is that the development is modifying what thoughts and thought production means in epistemology today. It is a development that is raising earnest questions on what it means to think today.

Is thinking reduced to only natural human thinking? Is memory reserved only to the faculties of the natural

---

[339] Pope Francis, "Place Man, Not Finance at Heart of Europe, Pope Tells Leaders," *Latest News*, 24th March 2017.

human mind? What constitutes the new mode of reasoning that is not natural, properly termed artificial intelligence (AI)? Could there be moral judgement or responsibility on what comes out from the reasoning of AI? For instance, a wrong interpretation of AI generated symbol like emoji today can rattle families and rock nations. So, what ethics guides AI senses and symbols? And are we outsourcing our minds and morals to something we created? Are we even becoming subjects and tools in the hands of machines made by our minds? These are provoking issues in epistemology today. This is why it is important that a study of epistemology explores what artificial intelligence is all about, and how it relates to the study of human knowledge and ethics in philosophical studies today.

Artificial Intelligence (AI) simply refers to the unnatural and non-human intelligence displayed by machines. It is somehow contrary to natural intelligence which has to do with human intelligence. AI is an offshoot of digital technology whereby machines are programmed to perform intelligent functions which, hitherto could have been performed by the human person. The operation of AI is possible through a technical systemization and manipulation of programmed data and algorithm. Data refers to the facts and statistics which are collected for computerised analysis and operations. Data (*datum*-singular) can be items, quantities, characters, representations, or symbols, etc, which are stored in computer memory and which the computer can send as electrical signals or magnetic or mechanical records. They can be used to create set of rules or procedure of operations called algorithm. This algorithm is used in handling calculation and computation of data from the computer memory. It is also used in digital problem-solving and creative generation of means to manage issues and development. The entire operations of the data collection and programs (algorithm) processes, which instruct and guide the computer on how to perform specific tasks or do some calculation or logical deductions is termed software (technology). This is different from hardware which refers to the mechanical system that makes the software operation to work.

However, it is significant to see that AI does not do an original thinking. It runs with data and algorithm created by natural human intelligence. It might produce logical output, but not human creative judgment. This is why its intelligence display is secondary and artificial as the name rightly captures it. It is a secondary product of human intelligence, deriving its logical intelligence through deductions from human primary intelligence. It may be capable of computational logical deduction, but it has no capacity of original logical illation. As a secondary order thinking, AI runs as a simulation or imitation of primary human intelligence. It is essentially a manufactured intelligence of a machine that could successfully perform intelligent functions that a human being performs. Writing on AI, Harry Katzan remarks that: "Artificial Intelligence is commonly regarded as the science of making machines do things that would require intelligence if performed by humans."[340] Alan Turing is remembered as first person to conduct special and sufficient research in computer studies and to project its capacity to perform intelligent functions. He termed the apparatus, a Machine Intelligence.[341] By

---

[340] Harry Katzan, *The Little Book of Artificial Intelligence* (Bloomington: iUniverse, 2021), 15.
[341] Cf. Jack Copeland, ed. *The Essential Turing: The Ideas that Gave Birth to the Computer Age* (Oxford: Clarendon Press, 2004),1ff.

1956, AI was made an academic discipline in schools, institutes of learning and universities. Thus, AI also means the field of study in computer science that is based on the understanding and development of intelligent machines. Today, it is a big industry and significant discipline in global academy and economy.

AI or software programmed data in algorithm is fast and accurate in logical thinking. It can perform inductive and deductive operations from the data fed into its memory, over a wide and various range of things. Its thinking is applied in healthcare, industrial activities, governmental administration, transport, farming, banking, commerce, education, research, religion etc. It can perform advanced and sophisticated operations like worldwide research and search of information (Google), commercial operations (sales, media provision), interpreting/understanding languages, super strategic analysis like computer games and creative functions like generation of articles and documentations as ChatGPT and AI art do.

There is also Narrow AI which perform specific tasks like language processing, and General AI which perform more versatile tasks. These AI operations though are simulations and imitations operate like semi human intelligence. Their intelligent products are near human in form and expression. They can solve human problems just like the human intelligence. The General AI for instance can learn, understand, and perform many intelligent functions like humans. Its General Intelligence operations execute human-like intelligent operations like reasoning, default reasoning, problem solving, knowledge representation/discovery, knowledge engineering, planning, learning, perception, natural language processing, clinical decision, robotic support, generative pre-trained transformer operations (GPT) etc. And it can complete these tasks performable by human beings in given time according to its algorithm.[342]

Of course, like human intelligence that needs to get inspiration from various experiences and memorial reservations, the Al takes or draws a lot of data from various aspects of human information. This is why it can combine its data base (memory) with information taken from various fields like linguistics, psychology, philosophy, neuroscience, machine learning, mathematics, logic etc to generate its intelligence (intelligent calculations or deductions). AI google for instance uses data from its "memorial" base to source answers, search for sites, calculate mathematical assignments, articulate discourses, reason out solutions, comparatively judge issues and intelligently offer (options for) decisions. It can solve human related problems and perform numerous human actions by intelligently searching through many workable solutions from its database, either by the "state space search" or the "local search."

In the AI technology, one sees the human effort to mechanize thinking whereby logical reasoning is outsourced to computation and automated theorem provers. An epistemologist can now engage the AI with declarative propositions, which the AI can handle through logical programming (prolog), to give him a procedural proposition that is logically sound and certifiable. Though the AI has approximated idea, its products are still epistemologically valid and dependable.

---

[342] Cf. Stuart J. Russell & Peter Norvig, *Artificial Intelligence: A Modern Approach,* 4th ed. (Hoboken: Pearson, 2021), 1:2.

But who takes the moral responsibility for the possible ideas that arise from human-AI synthetic knowledge production? Epistemological question as this is one of the reasons AI needs to form part of the study of human knowledge today. However, this challenge does not imply that epistemology and AI are in conflict or in contradictory relationship. They may have contrary approaches to human knowledge, but they still mediate and complement each other in one way or the other. For instance, both study epistemic relations of facts/data and propositions. The difference is that while artificial intelligence does that from the perspective of understanding formal and computational properties of frameworks, conventional epistemology does same by reflecting on the properties of their epistemic relations. The AI may focus on models of propositional relations of data while traditional epistemology would base its evaluation on conceptual properties of propositions.

It is important that AI and epistemology need not be studied in isolation considering the advanced information technology in the new world order. They have much in common. AI and analytical epistemology are so closely related that they need to form a synergy in the critical study of human knowledge today. Not primarily as interdisciplinary studies but as transdisciplinary studies on human knowledge. Of course, they have areas where each may excel the order, but they mediate each other. AI for instance may be dependent on fed data and prone to error if the data is false. It might be poor in originality or reasoning on circumstances and strange contexts unlike human intelligence. But its strength is in its wider data memory, speed, and certitude, considering its algorithm, which the human thinker and researcher need to function more accurately and faster too. This is why it is more adaptable and reliable to empirical knowledge reflections which require semantic, logical, mathematical, and calculable optimization.

AI may not have original innovativeness, but it can help human reasoning to widen information and logic while engaging in original reflection and creation of ideas. ChatGPT for instance might not be able to generate original ideas, but it can give a human thinker a wide range of ideas that can help his or her ideas come out brighter and richer. AI may not have the primary or common sense in thinking, but it is certainly not distracted or deviated by emotion in reasoning and making independent judgment as human reasoning is most likely to be. For a more dynamic and effective epistemology that strives towards increased efficiency, effectiveness, productivity, critical inquiry and deeper discovery, the assistance of AI technology may be necessary. This is why it needs to constitute a critical curve in epistemology in exploring the problems of human knowledge and issues or theories related to truth and its justification.

CONCLUSION

This work has examined the problems of human knowledge in diverse dimensions. It engaged the issues in both conventional and non-conventional streams of epistemology. The first and second parts of the work dwelt on critical discussions of the etymology, the definition, and the implications of human knowledge as justified true belief in classical epistemology. The definition and nature of human knowledge were examined using critical methods, especially that of Gettier. The questions and issues on how knowledge had always been defined as justified true belief were problematized by some vital challenges and discussions. But that is the authentic taste of the philosophy of knowledge, an ever-open operation that keeps the course dynamic and continuous. The third part examined human knowledge from a non-traditional or non-classical angle, as seen in the *Indigenous Knowledge Systems*, where human knowledge is viewed from a more volitive and existential perspective.

Studies on non-traditional systems of human knowledge are often seen as irrational and even magical by some scholars, especially those of a Western background. It is the effort to correct this wrong impression and judgment that this work delved into discussions on Igbo epistemology, which, until the recent times in the history of epistemology, has not been part of mainstream conventional studies in epistemology. For instance, the Igbo epistemic concept called *Akonuche* is neither magical nor irrational. Instead, it is an integrated epistemology which reconciles cognition (*ako/amamife*) and volition/conscience or goodwill (*uche*). It is a rational approach to humanizing what we know by either natural or artificial intelligence, whereby the ethics of knowing handles the lapses of technologies, terminologies, and methodologies associated with the problems of human knowledge. *Akonuche* opens a new order of epistemology embedded in a rich anthropological value system. Creating an awareness of this is one of the central goals of this work on the problems of human knowledge and theories of truth, thus inspiring a new way of thinking about knowledge and truth.

However, studying the various axes of human knowledge should be not just flexible, but engaging. There is no absolute truth in epistemology when discussing the truth of knowledge. The process of knowing may have an ultimate truth, but that is only sustained by the absence of new insight in the system. Beliefs will change form if a new insight shakes off the old one. The act of human knowing is always under construction, always dynamic, and changes with time and modifications of the circumstances of human anthropology and history.

For this reason, the dynamism of human knowing, and epistemology has shifted to new developments since the dawn of the digital age. The problems created by the deliberate production of ignorance (agnotology), conscious denial of truth in post-truth phenomena, and mechanized or digital thinking have changed the course's landscape. New developments are altering the regular grounds of epistemology, and new horizons are demanding new, inspiring perspectives for studying problems of human knowledge and truth.

This work, among others, aims to represent classical and non-classical epistemologies in order to respond to the urgent need for a more integrative epistemology in an age of globalization. Our age is highly conscious over wider issues, and new ways of perception and meaning can no longer be handled with a monolithic method. This is why the method of epistemology must change. It must have a novel approach rooted in traditional themes like the meaning of knowledge and theories of truth. At the same time, it has to accommodate non-traditional topics like ethno-epistemology, agnotology, and post-truth. The new epistemology method must also carry the epistemological attitude identifiable in the scholarship of the global North and the global South together. This is a significant point missing in how epistemology has been studied for many years. This innovative approach seeks comprehensiveness in the course. It seeks a more integrative epistemology in a new world order where encounters with new cultures and new capacities redefine the human person. The urgency of this need is paramount in the current global context, where diverse perspectives and knowledge systems are increasingly interconnected.

The integrative epistemology needed in our age must engage in a system of study of knowledge that seeks truth from various authentic sources to produce widespread richness. It must be a type of epistemology that firmly rejects polarization and the denigration of the finest thoughts based on prejudice and conflict that sometimes are found between some scholars of the global North and those of the global South. This rift is sometimes reflected in monolithic bibliographies and reference points of reflection or selection of materials for discussion in examining the problems of human knowledge. An integrative epistemology must permit a conversion of conceptualization with a potential for interdisciplinary and intercultural cross-pollination of ideas and values. It must be an epistemology that has to harness the rich meanings of our age and be open to broader heuristic experiences in examining what we know, what we choose to learn, and how what we know influences who we are and promotes our ideas and ideals. The need for such an integrative epistemology is not just a theoretical consideration but a practical necessity in our increasingly interconnected and diverse world.

Today's world needs an integrative epistemology that must re-invent a cross-cultural or transcultural scholarship where dialogue and convergence of enriching thoughts and values do not become isolated, thus avoiding a situation where specific thought patterns remain dogmatic. Such an integrative epistemology must contain and accommodate variances and newness to be creative and inventive while maintaining traditions of top thoughts. It must work with recognizing and integrating divergent structures of intelligence and diverse reasons, which can address the more profound questions facing the problems of human knowledge and truth in our time.

The discussions in this work should inspire options for the cultivation of the epistemic attitude that fits into what Robert Doran may describe as "psychic conversion,"[343] in the formation of human mind and knowledge system at large. Such a change of mind would bring in reflections on our common epistemic methodologies and faculties, respecting the diverse insights and interpretations from them. It must also reintegrate ideals and ideas that can create the emergence of richer answers to questions on human knowledge. It must create a new form of scholarship in which we think and operate beyond our space and place of experiences, to a wider cosmopolitan horizon through a process Bernard Lonergan describes as "perspectivism."[344] In this process one "acknowledges the truth of the many perspectives, …affirms the possibility of the many perspectives being joined together into a single fuller view."[345] Thus, making it possible for one to transcend one's subjectivity without losing it and be able to embrace

---

[343] By psychic conversion, Doran refers to openness to the reality of every moment, freedom from mechanical ties to the past, and static order. Cf. Robert Doran, *Subject and Psyche: Ricoeur, Jung, and the Search for Foundations* (Milwaukee: Marquette University Press 1994), 224.
[344] Cf. Lonergan, *Method in Theology*, 224.
[345] Bernard Lonergan, "History," in *Early works on Theological Method 1*, eds. Robert M. Doran and Robert C. Croken, CWL 22 (Toronto: University of Toronto Press, 2010), 248.

alternative viewpoints in his or her approach to truth.[346] Here, relative horizons, especially those compatible or "compossible"[347] to each other, must stream together to constitute a pool of perspectives that advance the search for solutions to the problems of *knowledge and truth.*

---

[346] Cf. Ani, *Critical History,* 175.
[347] Cf. Thomas J. McPartland, *Lonergan and the Philosophy of Historical Existence* (Columbia: University of Missouri, 2000), 65.

GLOSSARY

***Agnotology*-** is a term coined in 1992 by the Irish linguist, Iain Boal from two Greek terms: *ágnōsis* or *ágnōtos*– "not knowing", and *logia* "logic". It refers to deliberate cultural production of ignorance or doubt, by publication of inaccurate or misleading scientific data or disinformation.

***Akonuche*-** is a concept in Igbo epistemology and a composite term from *ako* (cognitive intelligence) and *uche* (thoughtfulness or wisdom). It literally means "knowledge with goodwill/conscience." Thus, refers to a moral mediation of human intelligence with conscience.

***Ako*-** is an Igbo epistemic term that means being wary, clever, discerning and cautious. It depicts the cognitive faculty, and sometimes shares similar meaning with the Igbo word, *amamife*.

***Amamife*-** is an Igbo epistemic concept that literary means knowledge, especially of things based on common sense perception or observation. It is related to *ako*, but they have subtle differences. *Amamife* satisfies the appropriation of propositional, logical, and functional knowledge.

***Alethia*-** is the Greek word that means "unconcealedness," of being or reality. It was first used by Parmenides in his poem, *On Nature* to differentiate truth from popular opinion (*doxa*). The term was later revived and used in the twentieth century existentialism by Martin Heidegger to explain "truth" as disclosure of being (*Dasein*), which is distinct from common concept of truth.

***Bullshitter*-** is a coinage by Harry Frankfurt in his book, *On Bullshit* to qualify the epistemic decadence of one with a post-truth mentality. The *Bullshitter* according to him does not care whether statements are true or false. He or she is indifferent to truth and lie, while making statements.

Consensus Gentium- is *Latin* phrase that simply means "agreement of the people." It is an ancient way of measuring truth as the universal consent of the people. Of course, this might be determined by the proportion of people that gave the consent and the period required to declare the consensus.

Dasein- is a German Heideggerian term that refers to "human existence." It was philosophically coined by Martin Heidegger to depict the mode of being in human existence as different from the mode of other beings/realities. *Dasein* is the being of humankind with self-awareness and who asks questions about its being and that of every being. In asking these questions, the *dasein* becomes the source of disclosure of the truth of every being.

Epistemicide- is derived from two Greek terms: *episteme* (knowledge or belief) and – *caedere* (to kill) or *cide* (killing). It literally means "killing knowledge or belief". It was coined and propagated by the Portuguese sociologist Boaventura de Sousa Santos, referring to the strategic destruction of existing knowledge system by some means and for some reasons.

Eziokwu- is the Igbo word for truth. It is a compound word made up of *ezi* (rightness/rectitude) and *okwu* (word or speech). It literally translates "right or correct word."

Igbo- is an ethnic group of the Southeastern Nigeria. *Igbo* also refers to the language of the same ethnic group, which belongs to the Niger-Congo language family in Africa.

Instrumentalism- is the term John Dewey used to describe his version of pragmatism. In this neologism of pragmatism, he holds that thinking is always instrumental in solving problems and transforming a practical situation. It is basically a problem-solving theory of truth and knowledge, whereby something is true if it helps one to survive and succeed through a precarious situation.

Nghota- is the Igbo translation of "understanding," which simply refers to proper cognition.

Nkwenye- is the Igbo translation of "belief," in an epistemic sense. It has an epistemological functionality that determines the nature of knowledge. *Nkwenye* is different from *okwukwe* which translates as "belief," but in a more religious sense.

Punctum Archimedis- literally translates as the "Archimedean point." It originated from the ancient classical scientist, Archimedes of Syracuse in Sicily who claimed that he could lift the earth off its foundation if given a solid place to stand out to form a lever. The expression is associated with a hypothetical point of view, strong enough for objective truth, otherwise called God's-eye view. Thus, a reliable stance for proper perception of reality, whereby one can reason independently for objectivity.

Quinque Viae- literary means "Five Ways," or "Five Proofs," which are the five logical arguments Thomas Aquinas posited to argue for the possible existence of God in his *Summa Theologica*. They include arguments from first mover, arguments from universal causation, arguments from contingency of being, arguments from degree and arguments from final cause or ends.

***Res cogitans*-** refers to the "thinking thing" according to Rene Descartes. It is the mental substance or nature of humans which is "unextended' as different from "extended things" (*res extensa*). The two form the substances in the ontology of Descartes. He used *res cogitans* to describe human nature that is conscious, doubts, understands, asserts, denies, is willing, is unwilling and has sense and imagination.

***STEM*-** is an acronym for Science, Technology, Engineering, and Mathematics. These four courses constitute the core studies in the natural sciences, and are based on innovation, technical problem-solving, and critical thinking. They are also known as hard skill knowledge, as different from soft skill knowledge.

***SOFT*-** skill courses focus on knowledge of basic Humanity studies like human relations, psychology, values, morality, vocational studies, philosophy, religion, and social issues.

***Uche*-**is the Igbo translation of the *mind* or power of "will" or "reason." It implies thoughtfulness and conscientious comprehension, whereby one exercises conscience and goodwill in understanding, judgment and decision.

BIBLIOGRAPHY

Ani, Humphrey Uchenna. *Introduction to Epistemology.* Enugu: PUKKA Press, 2023.

Ani, Humphrey Uchenna. *Critical History According to Bernard Lonergan.* Rome: Gregorian and Biblical Press, 2017.

Ani, Humphrey Uchenna. *Introduction to Philosophy of History.* Enugu: Snaap Press Ltd, 2021.

Ani, Humphrey Uchenna. *Introducing Philosophy to a Lay mind.* Enugu: Black Belt Konzult Ltd, 2008.

Ani, Humphrey Uchenna. *Discourses on Philosophy of History, A Study of Critical Conceptualizations on History.* Enugu: PUKKA Press, 2021.

Arendt, Hannah. "Truth and Politics." *The New Yorker*, February 25, 1967.

Arenson, K.W. "What Organizations Don't Want to Know Can Hurt." In *The New York Times*, 22nd August 2006.

Aristotle. *Metaphysics.* Edited by William D. Ross *Aristotle's Metaphysics*, vol. 1, Oxford: Clarendon Press, 1953.

Aquinas. *Summa Theologica.* Translated by Fathers of the English Dominican Province, New York: Benziger Brothers, Inc., 1948.

Aquinas. *Questiones Disputatae de Veritate*. Translated by Robert R. Mulligan. Chicago: Henry Regnery Company, 1952.

Audi, Robert. *Epistemology-A Contemporary Introduction to the Theory of Knowledge*. London: Routledge, 1998.

Austin, J. L. "Truth." *Philosophical Papers*, 3rd Edition. (1979): 117.

Bacon, Francis. *The Works of Bacon, Vol XIV*. Edited by James Spedding, Robert Leslie Ellis, and Douglas Denon Heath. Boston: Brown and Taggard, 1861.

Benton, Matthew. "Epistemology Personalized." *The Philosophical Quarterly* 67, no. 269 (2017): 813-834.

Bernardete, Seth. *The Being of the Beautiful*. Chicago: The University of Chicago Press, 1984.

Bittle, C.N. *Reality and the Mind*. New York: The Bruce Publishing Company, 1936.

Capps, John. "A Common-Sense Pragmatic Theory of Truth." In *Philosophia,* 48, no. 2 (2020): 463-481.

Cave, Peter. *How to Think Like a Philosopher*. Dublin: Bloomsbury Publishing Plc, 2023.

Chin, Cedric. *Thinking Better, The Four Theories of Truth as a Method for Critical Thinking* https://commoncog.com/four-theories-of-truth/

Chisholm, Roderick M. *Theory of Knowledge*. New Jersey: Prentice-Hall Inc. 1977.

Copeland, Jack. Editor. *The Essential Turing: The Ideas that Gave Birth to the Computer Age*. Oxford: Clarendon Press, 2004.

Copernicus, Nicholas. *On the Revolutions of the Celestial Spheres*. Cited by Jostein Gaarder, *Sophie's World, A Novel About the History of Philosophy*. Edited by Paulette Moller. New York: Berkley Books, 1991.

D'Ancona, Matthew. *Post-Truth: The New War on Truth and How to Fight Back*. London: Ebury Press, 2017.

Dancy, Jonathan. *A Companion to Epistemology*. Translated by Jonathan Dancy and Ernest Sosa. Malden: Blackwell Publishers Ltd, 1997.

Dallery, Arleen B, Charles E. Scott & Halley P. Robert. *Ethics and Danger: Essays on Heidegger and Continental Thought Issue, 17 of Selected Studies in Phenomenology and Existential Philosophy*. New York: State University of New York Press,1992.

De Chardin, Theilhard. *Man's Place in Nature*. London: Fontana/Collins Press,1974.

Descartes, Rene. "Meditations on First Philosophy." In *Descartes Philosophical Writings*. Translated and Edited by E. Anscombe and P.T. Geach. London: Nelson's University Paperbacks, 1975.

Dewey, John, *Logic: The Theory of Inquiry*. New York: Henry Hold and Company, 1938.

Dewey, John. *The Quest for Certainty: A Study of the Relation of Knowledge and Action*. New York: GP Putnam's Sons, 1929.

Dine, George Uchechukwu. *Traditional Leadership as Service Among the Igbo of Nigeria*. Rome: Laterenese University Press, 1983.

Doran, Robert. *Subject and Psyche: Ricoeur, Jung, and the Search for Foundations*. Milwaukee: Marquette University Press, 1994.

Eboh, Ben Okwu. *Basic Issues in the Theory of Knowledge*. Nsukka: Fulladu Publishing Company, 1995.

Eisen-Murphy, Claudia. "Aquinas on Voluntary Beliefs." *American Catholic Philosophical Quarterly*, 74(4), Fall 2000: 569–597.

Etta, Emmanuel E. and Asukwo Offiong. "The Reality of African Epistemology." In *International Journal of Innovative Science, Engineering & Technology*, Vol. 6, 279-305.

Frankfurt, Harry G. *On Bullshit*. Princeton: Princeton University Press, 1986.

Fricker, Miranda. "Epistemic Oppression and Epistemic Privilege." Canadian Journal of Philosophy, 29 (1999): 191–210.

Frise, Matthew. "Eliminating the Problem of Stored Beliefs." *American Philosophical Quarterly* 55, no 1 (2018): 63-79.

Hamlyn, D.W. *The Theory of Knowledge*. London: The Macmillan Press Ltd, 1977.

Gettier, Edmund L. "Is Justified True Belief Knowledge?" *Analysis* 23, no. 6 (1963): 121-123.

Gill, Jerry H. *Essays on Kierkegaard*. Minneapolis: Burgess Publishing Company, 1969.

Goldman, Alvin I. "Discrimination and Perceptual Knowledge." *The Journal of Philosophy* 73, no. 20 (1976): 771-791.

Hall, B.L. and R. Tandon. 'Decolonization of Knowledge, Epistemicide, Participatory Research and Higher Education.' in *Research for All*, 1 (1), (2017): 6–19.

Hamming, Bert. "Epistemology from the African Point of View." January 7, 2008,1.

Harter, Joel Harter. "Coleridge's Philosophy of Faith: Symbol, Allegory and Hermeneutics." *Religion in Philosophy and Theology* 55, no. x (2011): 1-242.

Hartman, Stephan. "Bayesian Epistemology." *The Routledge Companion to Epistemology*. London: Routledge, 2010.

Irikefe, Paul O. "African Epistemology." In *The Blackwell Companion to Epistemology, Third Edition*. Edited by Kurt Sylvan, Matthias Steup, Ernest Sosa, and Jonathan Dancy.

Iroegbu, Pantaleon. *Enwisdomizaiton and African Philosophy*. Owerri: International Universities Ltd, 1994.

Itohowo, Ignatius, Iniobong Umotong, Otto Dennis. "Heidegger's Notion of Truth as *Alethia*: A Critical Exposition." In *International Journal of Humanities and Innovation (IJHI)* Vol. 5 No. 2, (2022): 74-79.

James, William. "The Thing and its Relations." *Essays on Radical Empiricism*. Edited by William James. New York: Longman Green and Co, 1912: 92-122.

James, William. "Lecture 6: Pragmatism's Conception of Truth." In *Pragmatism: A New Name for Some Old Ways of Thinking*. Edited by William James. New York: Longman Green and Co.1907:76-91.

James, William. "Lecture 8: Pragmatism and Religion." In *Pragmatism: A New Name for Some Old Ways of Thinking*, 1907: 105-116.

James, William. "Pragmatism's Conception of Truth." In *Essays in Pragmatism*. Edited by Alburey Castell. New York: Hafner Press, 1948: 159-176.

Katzan, Harry. *The Little Book of Artificial Intelligence*. Bloomington: iUniverse, 2021.

Kenny, Anthony. *Aquinas on Mind*. New York: Routledge, 1993.

Kenyon, Georgina. "The Man Who Studies the Spread of Ignorance." In *BBC-Future News*, 6th January 2017.

Keyes, Ralph. *The Post-Truth Era: Dishonesty and Deception in Contemporary Life*. New York: St. Martin's Press, 2004.

Kierkegaard, Soren. *Concluding Unscientific Postscript: A Critical Guide*. Edited by Rick Anthony Furtak. New York: Cambridge University Press, 2010.

Kirkham, Richard. *Theories of Truth: A Critical Introduction*. Cambridge: MIT Press, 1992.

Kreitner, Richard. "Post-Truth and Its Consequences: What a 25-Year-Old Essay Tells Us About the Current Moment." In *The Nation*. 30 November 2016, Retrieved 1 December 2016.

Kreye, Andrian. "We Will Overcome Agnotology (The Cultural Production of Ignorance)." In *The Edge World Question Center*, 2007.

Lakatos, Imre. "Falsification and the Methodology of Scientific Research Programme." In *Philosophical Papers*. Cambridge: Cambridge University Press, 1978.

Lehrer, Keith. *Knowledge*. Oxford: Clarendon Press, 1974.

Levasseur, E. Robert. "People Skills: Developing Soft Skills—a Change Management Perspective." *Interfaces*. 43 (6) (2013): 566–571.

Liddell, Henry George & Robert Scott. *A Greek-English Lexicon at the Perseus Project*. Oxford: Clarendon Press, 1940.

Lonergan, Bernard. *Insight: A Study of Human Understanding*. Edited by F.E. Crowe and R. Doran, CWL, III. Toronto: University of Toronto Press, 1992.

Lonergan, Bernard. *Method in Theology*. Toronto: Toronto University Press, 1972.

Lonergan, Bernard. "History." In *Early works on Theological Method 1*. Edited by Robert M. Doran and Robert C. Croken, CWL XX. Toronto: University of Toronto Press, 2010.

Lynch, Michael. *Truth as One and Many*. Oxford: Oxford University Press, 2009.

McIntyre, Lee. *Post-Truth*. Cambridge: MIT Press, 2018.

McPartland, Thomas J. *Lonergan and the Philosophy of Historical Existence*. Columbia: University of Missouri, 2000.

Menand, Louis. *The Metaphysical Club: A Story of Ideas in America*. New York: Farrar, Straus, and Giroux, 2002.

Moore, George Edward. *Some Main Problems in Philosophy.* New York: Allen. & Unwin, 1953.

Nickerson, Raymond S. "Confirmation Bias: A Ubiquitous Phenomenon in Many Guises." *Review of General Psychology*, 2 (2) (1998): 175–220,

Offor, Francis. *Essentials of Logic.* Ibadan: Book Wright Publishers, 2014.

Oha, Obododimma. "Where Is *Ako*, Where Is *Uche*? In *Eke na Egwurugwu*, November 17, 2018.

Okere, Theophilus Okere. *Religion in a World of Change: African Ancestral Religion, Islam, and Christianity.* Aachen, North Rhine-Westphalia, Germany: Whelan, 2003.

Olsson, Erik J. "Bayesian Epistemology." *Introduction to Formal Philosophy* (2018): 431-442.

Omoregbe, Joseph. *Epistemology (Theory of Knowledge), A Systematic and Historical Study.* Lagos: Joja Press Limited, 1998.

Orwell, George. *Politics, and the English Language.* Peterborough: Broadview Press, 2006.

Otakpor, N. *Ezi Okwu Bu Ndu: Truth is Life.* Michigan City, IN: Hope Publications, 2008.

Patin, Beth. et al. "Interrupting Epistemicide: A Practical Framework for Naming, Identifying, and Ending Epistemic Injustice in the Information Professions." In SURFACE at Syracuse University School of Information Studies - Faculty Scholarship.

Peirce, Charles S. *The Philosophy of Peirce, Selected Writings.* Edited by Justus Buchler. Harcourt: Brace and Company,1960.

Peirce, Charles S. "The Founding of Pragmatism." *The Hound and Horn: A Harvard Miscellany* V. II, n. 3 (1929): 282-285.

Pettigrew, Richard. "Precis of Accuracy and the Laws of Credence." *Philosophy and Phenomenological Research* 96, no. 3 (2018): 749-254.

Plantinga, Alvin. *Warrant: The Current Debate.* New York: Oxford University Press, 1993.

Plato, "Meno." In *Classics of Western Philosophy.* Edited by Steven M. Cahn. Indianapolis: Hackett Publishing, 1977.

Plato. "Theaetetus." In *Plato: Complete Works*. Edited by John M. Cooper and D. S. Hutchinson. Indianapolis: Hackett Publishing Co., Inc., 1997.

Polanyi, Michael. "Tacit Knowing: Its Bearing on Some Problems of Philosophy." In *Reviews of Modern Physics*, 34 (4), October 1962: 601-606.

Pope Francis. "Place Man, Not Finance at Heart of Europe, Pope Tells Leaders." In *Latest News*, 24th March 2017.

Proctor, Robert. *Cancer Wars: How Politics Shapes What We Know and Don't Know About Cancer*. New York: Basic Books, 1995.

Proctor, Robert N and Londa Schiebinger. Editors. *Agnotology: The Making and Unmaking of Ignorance*. Stanford: Stanford University Press, 2008.

Quine, Willard and J.S. Ullian, *The Web of Belief*. New York: Random House, 1978.

Rooms, Nigel. "Paul as Practical Theologian: *Phronesis* in Philippians." In *Practical Theology*, (2012). 5:1, Published online 21 April 2015: 81-94.

Russell, Bertrand. *Human Knowledge: Its Scope and Limits*. London: George Allen and Unwin Ltd., 1948.

Russell, Bertrand. "On Denoting." *Mind.* 14, no. 56 (1905): 479-493.

Russell, Bertrand. "Knowledge by Acquaintance and Knowledge by Description." *Proceedings of the Aristotelian Society* 11, (1910): 108-128.

Russell, Bertrand. *Problems of Philosophy*. Edited by John Perry. Oxford: Oxford University Press, 1912.

Russell, Bertrand. *Philosophical Essays*. London: Longmans, Green and Company, 1910.

Russell, Stuart J. & Peter Norvig. *Artificial Intelligence: A Modern Approach, 4th Edition.* Hoboken: Pearson, 2021.

Ryle, Gilbert. "Knowing How and Knowing That-The Presidential Address." In *Meeting of the Aristotelian Society at the University of London Club on November 5th, 1945, at 8, pm.*

Sahakian, William & Mabel Lewis Sahakian. *Ideas of the Great Philosophers*. New York: Barnes and Noble,1865https://archive.org/details/ideasofgreatphil00will0/page/3.

Sanborn, Patricia F. *Existentialism*. New York: Pegasus, 1968.

Santos, Boaventura de Sousa, *Epistemologies of the South, Justice Against Epistemicide*. Edited by Maria Paula Meneses. New York: Routledge, 2014.

Skyrms, Brian. "The Explication of 'X knows that p.'" *The Journal of Philosophy* 64 no. 12 (1967): 373-389.

Spivak, Gayatri Chakravorty. "Can the Subaltern Speak?" In *Two Works Series Volume One*. Edited by Amber Husain and Mark Lewis. Koln: Afterall Books, 2021.

Stanley, Jason, and Timothy Williamson. "Knowing How." *Journal of Philosophy*, 98 (8) 2001: 411–444.

Stumpf, Samuel Enoch & James Fieser. *Philosophy, History and Problems, Seventh Edition*. New York: McGraw-Hill, 2008.

Succi, Chiara Succi, "Soft Skills for the Next Generation: Toward a Comparison between Employers and Graduate Students' Perceptions." *Sociologia del Lavoro*. 137: 244–256.

Talbert, Bonnie. "Knowing Other People." *Ratio* 28, no. 2 (2015): 190-206.

Tarski, Alfred. "The Semantic Conception of Truth." In *Philosophy and Philosophical Research*, 4 (1944): 342-376.

Tesich, Steve. "A Government of Lies." *The Nation*, January 6, 1992.

Thomas, Helen. "Indigenous Knowledge Is Often Overlooked in Education. But It Has a Lot to Teach Us." in *Edsurge*.

Tool, Marc. "John Dewey." In Elgar Companion to Institutional and Evolutionary Economics 1. Edited by G.M. Hodgson. Northampton: Edward Elgar Publishing, 1994.

Udefi, Amechi. "Theoretical Foundations for an African Epistemology." In *Footprints in Philosophy*. Edited by R. A. Akanmidu. Ibadan: Hope Publications Ltd, 2005:74-75.

Udefi, Amaechi. "The Rationale for an African Epistemology: A Critical Examination of the Igbo Views on Knowledge, Belief, and Justification." In *Canadian Social Science*, 10 (3), (2014): 108-117. http://www.cscanada.net/index.php/css/article/view/4445.

Uduigwomen, Andrew. "The Place of Oral Tradition in African Epistemology." In *Footmarks on African Philosophy*. Lagos: O. O. P. 1995.

Viglino, Ugo. *La Conoscenza*. Roma: Pontificia Universitas Urbaniana, 1969.

Warburton, Nigel. "Truth by Consensus." In *Thinking from A to Z*. London: Routledge, 2000.

West, J. A. "Aquinas on Intellect, Will, and Faith." in *Aporia* Vol. 13 number 1—2003.

Whitehead, Alfred North. *Essays in Science and Philosophy*. London: Rider and Cole, 1948.

Williams, David R. "Venus Fact Sheet." *NASA Goddard Space Flight Center*. Archived from the original on 11 May 2018. Retrieved 15 April 2021.

Williams, John N. "Belief-in and Belief in God." *Religious Studies* 28, no. 3 (1992): 401-406.

Wiredu, Kwasi. *Philosophy and an African Culture*. Cambridge: Cambridge University Press, 1980.

Wright, Crispin. *Truth and Objectivity*. Cambridge: Harvard University Press, 1992.

Yuval Noah Harari. "Yuval Noah Harari Extract: 'Humans are a Post-Truth Species.'" *The Observer*, August 5, 2018.

Zubairi, Naseem B. "African Heritage and Contemporary Life: An Experience of Epistemology Change." www.cnp.orgU30T Accessed. December 20, 2008.

The Author

Dr. Humphrey Uchenna Ani, who hails from Egede, in the state of Enugu, Nigeria, is a Catholic Priest of the Enugu diocese, and a Lonergan Fellow at Boston College, Boston, Massachusetts. His intellectual prowess is evident in his academic achievements, including a first-class in his doctorate studies in Philosophy from the Jesuit Pontifical Gregorian University, Rome. He has also studied Philosophy, Theology, and Religion at Seat of Wisdom Seminary, Owerri, Imo State, an affiliate of Pontifical Urban University, Rome, and Imo State University, Owerri.

His commitment to personal and professional growth is exemplified by his enrollment in a postgraduate marketing course at the University of Nigeria, Nsukka (Enugu Campus), where he is dedicated to honing his expertise and expanding his knowledge in the field. In addition to his current research, Fr. Ani is the author of *Introducing Philosophy to a Lay-Mind* (2008), *Tim Buckley, The Story of a Missionary Legend'* (2008), *Critical History According to Bernard Lonergan* (2017), *Topics in Epistemology*

(2019), *Introduction to Philosophy of History* (2021), *Discourses on Philosophy of History* (2021), and *Introduction to Epistemology* (2023). Ani's leadership roles include being a senior Lecturer and the Head of the Department of Philosophy at Bigard Memorial Seminary Enugu, where he also lectures on Epistemology, Philosophy of History, and Introduction to Philosophy. Dr. Ani is the same as the Bigard Lonergan Research Institute Director at Bigard Memorial Seminary, Enugu.

Currently, Dr. Ani is a professor of philosophy at Saint John Vianney College Seminary in Miami, Florida, where he inspires students with his passion for deep thinking through his lectures on Logic and Epistemology.

www.ingramcontent.com/pod-product-compliance
Lightning Source LLC
Chambersburg PA
CBHW021838220426
43663CB00005B/303